HAPPY HOMEMAKING

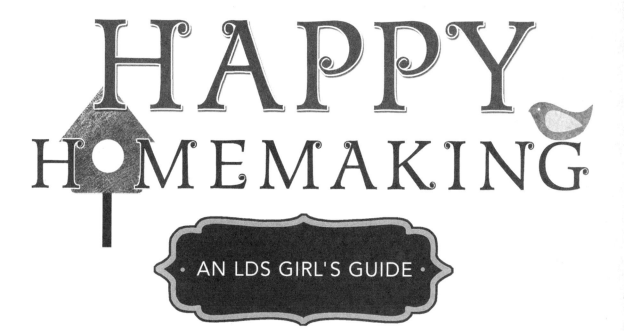

AN LDS GIRL'S GUIDE

ELYSSA ANDRUS AND **NATALIE HOLLINGSHEAD**

CFI

AN IMPRINT OF CEDAR FORT, INC.

Springville, Utah

To Dave, Tyler, Lily and Josh: I am happiest at home because of you.

ELYSSA

To my husband and children: What I love most about my home is who I share it with.

NATALIE

ISBN 13: 978-1-4621-1101-5
Published by CFI, an imprint of Cedar Fort, Inc.
2373 W. 700 S., Springville, UT 84663
Distributed by Cedar Fort, Inc., www.cedarfort.com

LIBRARY OF CONGRESS CATALOGING-IN-PUBLICATION DATA

Andrus, Elyssa, 1978- author.
  Happy homemaking : an LDS girls' guide / Elyssa Andrus and Natalie Hollingshead.
    pages cm
  Includes bibliographical references and index.
  ISBN 978-1-4621-1101-5 (alk. paper)
  1. Home economics--Handbooks, manuals, etc. 2. Home--Religious aspects--Church of Jesus Christ of Latter-day Saints. I. Hollingshead, Natalie, 1983- author. II. Title.

  TX158.A56 2012
  745.5--dc23

              2012016335

Cover and interior design by Erica Dixon
Cover design © 2012 by Lyle Mortimer
Edited and typeset by Whitney A. Lindsley

Printed in the United States of America

10 9 8 7 6 5 4 3 2 1

Printed on acid-free paper

CONTENTS

·INTRODUCTION·

A few years ago, I made ridiculously gorgeous bread pudding to take to my in-laws' for Christmas Eve dinner. This yearly event is always a fancy, formal affair, so I was trying to show off. My mother-in-law raised ten children and is the kind of amazing woman who sewed her children's jeans and could probably butcher a hog with a kid on one arm. She was always giving me recipes for dishes so easy "anyone could make them." I knew she wasn't being intentionally patronizing, but the message was clear: Here is a recipe so easy even a monkey could do it.

She has a point. I certainly don't come by culinary talent. I come from a line of mostly working women who have relied on drive-thrus and dry cleaning to cover up a lack of domestic skills. My own mother didn't work outside the home, but she was up to her eyeballs in children. She has eleven, three of whom are still at home. She loved us, played with us, let us trash her house with construction paper and glitter-glue, and at mealtime defrosted frozen pizza and mozzarella sticks. I witnessed everything there is to learn about being a Christlike, loving mother by watching her, but somehow we never got around to pie-making.

Not that I would have paid attention. Before leaving for college, my path was clear: I was going to get an education, have a career. My multitude of servants could attend to balancing my books, scouring my baseboards, and deboning the chicken. I was going to be busy and important and famous.

Fast-forward sixteen years. I have a master's degree in journalism from Northwestern University. I have a career as a newspaper editor. I also have a husband and three very hungry young children who could care less about my vast knowledge of punctuation. In fact, if they really knew how much I knew about commas, they would hate me for it. My army of servants has yet to materialize, so I'm left to budget, sew, and cook on my own, despite the education and career.

And a part of me likes to think that even if I had a household staff of pastry chefs fighting over whose turn it was to make the chocolate cake, I would want to do it myself anyway. There is something extraordinarily satisfying about slathering a from-scratch cake with homemade buttercream frosting. After all, they won't let you lick the bowl at Walmart.

Latter-day Saint Church leaders have long counseled their membership on self-reliance and provident living. I believe every young woman today needs an employable skill that will allow her to support herself and family should she need to at various times of her life. I also believe that it's crucial for young men and women to embrace the Church's provident living counsel and learn the financial and domestic skills that allow for a richly lived, self-reliant life.

If the Great Recession has taught me anything, it's that thrift, industry, and homemaking never go out of style. Who needs to be able to balance a budget, sew on a button, or plant a garden? Everyone, really, regardless of age, income, or gender.

About the time I had to serve hot dogs to my two kids for every meal, I decided I had better learn, on a basic level, how to cook. We couldn't afford to eat out every night, and I really didn't want my kids having the glut of high-calorie, high-fat foods.

What started as an attempt to learn the difference between sauté and flambé has evolved into a broader quest to acquire the basic domestic skills I think many of my generation either scorned or overlooked. And I'm trying to do it in a sane, semi-realistic way. I'm never going to be Martha Stewart. As much as I love the idea of crisp linens, I have neither the time nor the energy to iron my bed sheets every day.

To cowrite this book, I recruited fellow journalist Natalie Hollingshead. We met in 2004, when Natalie began writing freelance for the daily newspaper where I work as an editor. In conversations over the years, we discovered a mutual interest in provident living and domestic know-how, although she comes by it a bit more naturally than I do.

Natalie learned most of what she knows about running a household from watching her mother, a woman who has never opened a box of Hamburger Helper and refuses to serve cold cereal when time allows for homemade biscuits, bacon, and eggs. When her five children lived at home, she made nearly everything from scratch: birthday cakes and cookies, Halloween costumes and window cleaner.

Fortunately, Natalie inherited her mother's zeal for the art of homemaking. She grinds wheat, bottles applesauce, and dusts religiously. And while she occasionally takes things a bit too far—like the time she hand-sewed individual capes for all of the guests at her son's superhero birthday party—she, like me, is most interested in provident living and homemaking skills that are really doable. Because as much as Natalie loves sewing, cooking, decorating, and really anything that can be made into a to-do list, she happily accepts shortcuts here and there. One-hour bread recipe? Check. Iron-on hem tape? Check. Drive-thru dinner in an emergency? Check and check.

In the coming chapters, "we" refers to Natalie and me. "You" is talking to, well, you. Stories specific to individual experiences will say Elyssa or Natalie.

Please understand that this book isn't going to teach you how to tile your backsplash. It won't touch on origami for place settings or how to fold your napkins into swans for dinner parties. But it will explore basic domestic skills, including how to make killer dish or two for said dinner parties—like the bread pudding I made for Christmas Eve dinner.

The pudding really was so gorgeous, the bread a golden brown atop dark, bubbling raspberries. I had this overwhelming feeling of pride as I pulled it out of the oven. It was almost a look-how-far-I've-come moment, a testament that with lots of faith and hard work—and a little luck—even a city girl like me could channel her inner pioneer.

I was so giddy at these thoughts that I failed to notice I had set the pudding on a hot burner on the stove. I walked away for a minute, only to be pulled back into the kitchen by the sound of shattering glass. The pan exploding was like something out of an action movie. It sent shards of glass and hunks of bread and raspberries flying clear into the family room. If I didn't know better, I would have thought a crime had been committed. But I did know better, and so I laughed hysterically, hyena-like, thinking that the moment was straight out of some eighties Christmas comedy. And then I cried. A lot.

Becoming a domestic diva is a process, and there's bound to be some burnt bread in the process. (Or, in my case, exploding bread pudding.) But the important thing is to get started, to try, and to take both the successes and failures for what they are: part of the learning experience. I still get nervous when I hear the phrase "reduction sauce," but at some point you just have to be a woman—or man—about it and figure out how to thread your sewing machine or scrub your microwave or take a good, honest look at your finances.

I figure if I can do it, so can you. If it helps, imagine my sweet mother-in-law whispering in your ear, "Creating a budget is so easy, anyone can do it," "Planting tomatoes is so easy, anyone can do it," or "Making this recipe is so easy, anyone can do it." She's right, you know.

IN THE MONEY
Family Finances

When you think homemaking, you think . . . budgeting? It might surprise you, but learning to manage your finances is a crucial domestic skill. In fact, it's perhaps the most important one. Smart money management will allow you to someday own a home, to comfortably care for the children you do or may have, to pursue things you are passionate about, to help and serve others, and to enjoy life.

Regardless of age or income level, everyone has to think about money. Maybe you are like Elyssa's brother Jared, who has two sets of young twins and is trying to figure out a way to pay for medical school and basic expenses like food and clothing. Maybe you are a society heiress who uses dollar bills as tissue to remove your eye makeup. It doesn't matter. To live richly and well, everyone needs financial goals, planning, and a budget. It's an essential part of provident living.

In 2007, The Church of Jesus Christ of Latter-day Saints issued the pamphlet *All Is Safely Gathered In: Family Finances*. It includes this First Presidency statement: "We encourage you wherever you may live in the world to prepare for adversity by looking to the condition of your finances. We urge you to be modest in your expenditures; discipline yourselves in your purchases to avoid debt. . . . If you have paid your debts and have a financial reserve, even though it be small, you and your family will fee more secure and enjoy greater peace in your hearts."[1]

Smart family finances provide a crucial base for any well-run household. It doesn't matter that you know how to shop sales at the grocery store if you are constantly splurging on expensive restaurant dinners. And knowing how to sew on a button won't help your pocketbook if you have a weakness for luxury goods. You need to know how much money you are bringing in, how much you are spending, and what you want to do with anything that's left over. It may sound tedious and time consuming, but once you have the hang of it, money management can be thrilling. In a word, it's *awesome*.

For most of the first decade of her marriage, Elyssa spent money haphazardly, with no regard to what was coming or going. Her credit card was frequently declined. She didn't really know why, but she was pretty sure it was her husband's fault. One of her favorite questions for him was, "Why don't we ever have any money?" She was convinced it was all going to a secret snowmobile fund in an off-shore bank. It had to be, right?

Then one day her husband made her sit down and actually look at their credit card statement. The most striking thing was she couldn't pinpoint any big-ticket "secret" purchases. It was ten dollars at McDonald's here, fifty dollars at Target there. And it added up in all the wrong ways.

Interestingly, it was a series of financial firesides in her LDS ward that really got Elyssa thinking about smart money management. These firesides focused on basic principles such as budgeting and getting out of debt, and they inspired Elyssa to start spending less and saving more. Hopefully, this book will do the same for you, because devising a solid financial plan early on will set you up for a lifetime of success.

One great thing about planning and budgeting is that you can spend money on what's meaningful and important to you, without any of the guilt that comes from undisciplined shopping. When Natalie and her husband, Todd, married, Todd was a natural saver. He just couldn't bear to spend money. At all. Creating a budget was empowering for the couple, because they realized that they were saving enough each month that they could afford to have some fun too. So if you really want to take a vacation, buy a house, or save up for that new iPhone, read on. We'll tell you how to do it.

To write this chapter, we consulted John Brandt, the financial aid director and an adjunct professor of business at Southern Virginia University, a liberal arts college that embraces the values of Latter-day Saint students.[2] Brandt has a master of business administration in finance, has raised six children, and serves as bishop of a young single adult ward in Buena Vista, Virginia. He knows a thing or two about finances and young people. Below are some of his suggestions for getting your financial house in order.

• IT'S UP TO YOU •

Brandt said that twenty or thirty years ago, many companies offered pensions that provided employees with money to live on after they retired. And the US society had some safety nets in place in the event that people ran into trouble or needed help, such as the welfare program and Social Security. During our challenging economic times, fewer companies provide full pensions for their employees. And the rising generation may not be able to count on income from Social Security and other government-run programs, says Brandt. In other words, it's up to you to plan for your financial future, including retirement, now.

• WHO NEEDS MONEY, ANYWAY? •

Well, we all do. It certainly won't buy you happiness, and being fixated on wealth and money is a sure way to live an empty, unhappy life. But smart money management and financial security allow us to heed President Thomas S. Monson's request to care for the poor and needy. If we are able to acquire some level of wealth, then we can use that money to help those around us. And in our quest for financial security, it's important to put the Lord first by paying an honest tithe. (More on that later.)

• GENERATING INCOME •

There are two key financial components every individual or family must address: Money coming in (revenue) and money going out (expenses). It's pretty basic, but the key to smart money management is to have more money coming in than going out.

When you think about finances, it's easy to get caught up in the pinching pennies and budgeting end of the equation. That's an important component, sure, but an equally important part—or even more important—is to secure a good income. And the way to do that is to find something you love, something you are passionate about, something you can put your heart and sweat into, says Brandt.

Now is the time to pursue your dreams and obtain an education. Even women who plan to be stay-at-home moms will likely have to support themselves at some point in their lives. Even if you're not the main breadwinner, it's nice to be able to do something to supplement primary income, like teaching piano or helping people with their taxes or writing technical manuals from home.

Having an employable skill is crucial. Now is also the time to start looking for ways to generate passive income, or income that you make without working additional hours. This type of income can come in the form of interest earned in a savings account, from a rental property, or from other investments. "The idea is to generate passive income so that you aren't a slave to your time," says Brandt.

• THREE DOCUMENTS EVERYONE NEEDS •

Once you've thought long and hard about how you and your family will make enough money to live on, it's time to start thinking about expenses. Brandt suggests having three documents to help manage your finances: a financial goals worksheet, a budget, and a balance sheet. Let's look at each one in a little more detail.

✐ FINANCIAL GOALS WORKSHEET

This can be any piece of paper you (and if you are married, your spouse) use to plan out your financial goals for the future. It should include short-term goals (things done in a year), intermediate goals (in one to five years), and long-term goals (anything over five years). These goals should be as specific and include a time frame for accomplishing them, says Brandt. For example, instead of saying, "I want to save for retirement," say, "I want to save X amount of dollars by the time I reach age sixty-five, so I can make fifty thousand dollars a year for the rest of my life without working." Some of these goals could include

- ❧ How much income you would like to generate and how you plan to do so

- ❧ What kinds of charitable contributions you would like to make in addition to tithing

- ❧ How much you plan to put into savings per month and per year

- ❧ How much you plan to save for retirement

- ❧ When and how you plan to purchase a home

- ❧ What big-ticket items (such as a car or a vacation) you would like to save for

Goal setting and evaluating is an exercise that can be done quarterly, says Brandt.

✐ BUDGET

A budget is simply a monthly plan that should tell you how each cent of your take-home pay should be spent. It can be as low-tech as a few columns jotted down on a piece of paper, or as tech-savvy as an online computer program that tracks your expenses for you. (Some popular online money management sites are Mint.com and Quicken.com. The LDS Church also has a simple, user-friendly budgeting worksheet in the *All Is Safely Gathered In: Family Finances* pamphlet on its Provident Living website: www.providentliving.org.)

At the end of the day, you need your income and expenses to balance out. We find it most helpful to plug in the number of dollars we have per month AFTER tithing, fast offerings, retirement savings, and taxes have already been taken out. We also have "additional savings" as our first "spending" category, knowing that we will save a certain percentage of our take-home pay each month. Brandt suggests that people put at least 10 percent of their income toward savings and to put 20 percent or more away if possible. Some spending categories will be fixed, such as housing (rent or mortgage), insurance, and utilities, while others, such as food, gifts, and entertainment, have more leeway. But it's important to know that there are few true "fixed" expenses in a budget. If your rent is too expensive, you may need to find a new place to live. If you can't afford gas for your car, you could look into public transportation. The key is to make sure that you are spending less than you earn, with money left over for savings.

Establishing a budget is the easy part. Sticking to it is the challenge. To do so, you need to track your spending in each of your categories. You can save receipts and manually write down your expenditures, or some online programs will do the work for you. In the beginning, it may be helpful to track all of your spending yourself (instead of letting a computer program do it for you) because it's much easier to be accountable for your spending when you physically record it. Some budgeting experts even recommend you put cash in different envelopes for all your spending categories. That way, when the money is gone, you can't spend any more. This is a compelling exercise that may be useful for people who have had a hard time sticking to a budget in the past. The drawback to this method, however, is that cash can be lost or stolen, especially when you are dealing with large sums of it.

However you choose to track spending, it's important to assess your progress weekly and see where you are for each spending category and what adjustments you need make to stay on budget. Natalie and her husband, for example, usually have a quick budget update after family home evening.

You should evaluate your budget worksheet at the beginning of every month as well because it may need some tweaking depending on what you have planned. If, for example, you know you will be taking a road trip during the month, you may need to budget a bit more in the transportation category and cut back on another adjustable category, such as entertainment.

"A budget is a living document, so your circumstances are going to change over time," says Brandt. "A budget is a tool to help you achieve your financial goals; that's what it is. As you look at your budget, see what you have been able to accomplish and what you haven't. If you aren't making progress toward your goals, it's time to readjust that process and make sure it's happening."

Brandt says it's also important to go through your banking statements monthly to look for any errors that may have been made by you, a company you patronized, or your bank. Online banking and technology such as smart phones make this possible to do with a click of a button. And catching a problem early on—such as a stolen credit or debit card—can save you a mountain of hassle and heartache.

❧ FINANCIAL BALANCE SHEET

The third document Brandt suggests young people have is a financial balance sheet. This lists your assets (things that are worth money) and your liabilities (your debts) to give you a true big-picture look at your net worth. On the assets side may be things like savings accounts and checking accounts, retirement accounts, rental properties, cars, and real estate. The liabilities are what you owe other people and might include things such as a mortgage or a car loan. To find your net worth, subtract your liabilities from your assets. Obviously, what remains should be a positive number. The more assets and fewer liabilities you have, the better financial shape you are in. The balance sheet is an annual exercise you can participate in, says Brandt, to gauge your overall financial health.

• PROTECT YOURSELF •

Once you've established financial goals, set a budget, and looked at your financial big picture, it's time to minimize financial risk in your life by creating a few safety nets. "What are the things that could absolutely destroy you from a financial perspective?" asks Brandt. An accident, illness, or job loss could be a huge financial setback, but there are things you can do to minimize your risk.

Here are a couple of things Brandt recommends doing to protect yourself:

First, determine your insurance needs. If you own a driver's license and drive a car, most states mandate that you carry automobile insurance. Make sure that you carry enough liability insurance, so you will be saved from financial ruin in the event of an accident. You should also purchase appropriate health insurance if you are not a student covered under your parents' plan. In addition to car and health insurance, if you are married, you should consider life insurance. This is necessary once you have children, says Brandt. There are various formulas for figuring how much life insurance you will need, but an easy calculation is to purchase six to ten times your annual income. Most experts recommend purchasing life insurance for stay-at-home moms as well.

Second, establish an emergency fund. In the past, financial experts have recommended that people save enough money to cover three to six months of living expenses. This critical fund would help in the event of a job loss, serious illness, or other financial hardship, and would hopefully help you avoid relying on relatives, the Church, or the government to meet expenses until employment is secured again. Brandt says that, in today's economy, it may take someone more than three to six months to find a job. For this reason, he recommends establishing an emergency fund to cover six to twelve months of expenses. (Remember, this fund represents expenses, the basic amount you would need to live on each month, not income.) If you haven't begun to establish this fund, make it one of your top priorities.

Build adequate food storage. Extra nonperishable food is another safety net that can protect you in times of financial difficulty or crises. Establishing adequate food storage will be discussed at length in chapter six.

• DEALING WITH DEBT •

Debt is bad. Except when it isn't. In some cases, debt can be okay and even necessary. You may need to go into debt to buy a modest home, to secure an education, to start a business, or to pay for other crucial needs. But debt—especially consumer debt used to pay for luxury items and unnecessary "wants"—can create a cycle of bondage and despair. In an October 1979 general conference address, N. Eldon Tanner, then a member of the First Presidency of The Church of Jesus Christ of Latter-day Saints, said: "Those who structure their standard of living to allow a little surplus, control their circumstances. Those who spend a little more than they earn are controlled by their circumstances. They are in bondage."[3]

If you are already in debt beyond a mortgage or perhaps a student loan, and particularly with unpaid credit card balances, it's time to get your financial house in order by establishing a strict budget and saving money to start paying off what's owed. You can use a debt-elimination calendar, readily available online, to help you. The calendar can be a powerful tool, but more important is learning to control your need to spend.

• I WANT IT . . . LATER •

Easily one of the most compelling characters in the 1971 movie *Willy Wonka and the Chocolate Factory* is Veruca Salt, a hyper-spoiled child who stomps around the chocolate factory, screaming "I want it now!" about, well, everything. On some level, we can probably all relate to her. Who wants to wait for a new car when the one you are driving has ripped leather seats, a weak air conditioner, and smells funny? And who wants to wait for new living room furniture when you are using hand-me-downs from your grandma that were last in style in the sixties? It's especially hard to save for the things you want when credit is easily available. Your neighbor has a new boat, and your sister has a new car, and even that kid who delivers pizza down the road has a new iPad. Why shouldn't you?

It is human nature to want nice, new things, and it really does take effort and sacrifice to put off purchases until you can afford them. If there is one good thing to come from the US financial crisis that began in 2007, it's that many people are starting to embrace the good, old-fashioned values of thrift and industry. Americans are starting to save more and to learn to live with less. And that's a good thing. As mentioned above, debt can create a cycle of misery and despair. On the other hand, only buying what you can truly afford comes with something you can't put a price on: peace of mind.

We'll talk at length about this in chapter ten (organizing), but sometimes the best thing to do when you think you need to buy something—anything—is to wait it out. If you are itching to purchase something, wait a day; wait a week if you can. So many times, once the initial impulse to buy passes, you realize you didn't need that thing after all. Or perhaps you can borrow the item or buy it used.

If, as time goes by, you still feel like you need something, then when you have saved enough and can pay cash for the item, you'll know it's a worthwhile purchase. For example, when Elyssa entered her first sprint triathlon, she wanted to buy a road bike for the biking portion of the competition. But road bikes can cost upwards of one thousand dollars—a pretty steep price for a casual race. She asked around, and instead of purchasing a bike, she was able to borrow one from a friend for the race day. And she was also able to find several local bike shops that would have rented her the bike for around thirty-five dollars.

Or, like Natalie and her husband, you may save cash for an item and decide to put it toward another goal instead. Every year, the couple declares "This is the year!" to replace the fuzzy and hard-to-hear twenty-seven-inch television they were handed down as newlyweds. But every year, they have put off purchasing a new TV in favor of putting the money toward a vacation instead. Someday they will upgrade. For now, it is nice to know that life moves forward without a forty-six-inch HDTV.

The beauty of a cooling-off period for purchases is that it takes emotion out of the equation and allows you to evaluate each purchase from a logical standpoint. Of course, this mandated waiting period might mean that you occasionally miss one-time opportunities and sales. And that's okay. If you do, tell yourself it wasn't meant to be, and enjoy the comfort that comes from making smart purchasing decisions.

✍ CREDIT CARDS

Credit cards can be a great convenience, allowing you to track purchases and to make them without having to carry large sums of cash. But they also represent a great temptation, says Brandt. It takes careful self-discipline to pay them off in full every month. A debit card, a piece of plastic similar to a credit card that automatically deducts money from a checking account, affords some of the same protection and convenience as a credit card, but without the same enticements to overspend.

⟨ • GO FORWARD AND SAVE • ⟩

Now that you have all the financial tools in place, it's time to spend wisely and carefully. Although living frugally isn't the only component to smart money management, it's an important one. To save money, you must spend less on the things you need and want. Here are some suggestions for pinching your pennies. Note that some suggestions are discussed in more detail in other chapters.

✍ LIVING SPACE AND UTILITIES

Don't be house (or apartment!) poor. Before you sign an apartment lease or purchase a home, make sure that you can actually afford to live there. Remember that the rent or a mortgage payment won't be the only expense associated with the place you live. In an apartment or rental, you may need to pay for things like utilities and renter's insurance in addition to the rental price. For a home, you'll need to factor in items such as homeowner's insurance, utilities, maintenance and repairs, a homeowner's association fee (if you live in community that requires one), and taxes.

Be temperature savvy. Save money on utilities by keeping the thermostat no higher than 70°F (21°C) in the winter, and no lower than 76°F (24°C) in the summer. If possible, install a programmable thermostat to regulate the temperature at night and when you aren't home.

Make your living space energy efficient by installing compact fluorescent light bulbs (CFLs) and energy-efficient, low-emissivity (Low-E) windows.

Use your dryer less. If it's possible to hang your clothes on a line outside during the summer, there's no better way to dry clothes. If that's not an option, install hooks in your home to hang clothes that will dry quickly, using the dryer for bigger items such as sheets. This will also extend the life of your clothing, and it's especially important to let items you don't want to shrink air-dry. (See chapter eight on clothing care for more information.)

Run full loads of laundry and dishes to maximize the water you are saving. Watch your time in the shower and the number of baths you take to cut down on your water bill.

If you have a cell phone, do you need to pay for a home phone as well? Elyssa doesn't have a home phone and loves no longer worrying about calls from solicitors. If you need a home phone—Natalie does so she can affordably talk to her family in Canada—look into bundling your phone, cable, and Internet service for extra savings.

Along those lines, do you really need cable? A lot of television shows can be watched on the Internet, and canceling cable may motivate you to be more productive, read more, learn another language, run for president, or whatever. If you feel that you want cable or satellite, talk to your provider about available packages and see if you can lower the bill. You may not even miss the thirty different sporting channels you end up losing.

❧ TRANSPORTATION

Drive less or not at all. Depending on the area where you live, can you get by with a bicycle or a bus pass? If you are married and have two cars, do you really need both of them? Even if you want to drive some of the time, the simple acts of taking public transportation, bicycling, or carpooling when possible will give your wallet some room to breathe.

If you do own a car, maintain it well. Check your owner's manual to see how often the vehicle calls for an oil change, tire rotation, and other basic maintenance that can extend the life of your car.

Periodically check to make sure that your tires are properly inflated. Under-inflated tires can waste gasoline, and tires not set to the right pressure will wear out more quickly.

When something is wrong, fix it fast. Don't let a minor mechanical problem snowball into something more by ignoring it. This is especially important with your brakes. If they start to squeal or feel different from normal in any way, act immediately.

Drive smart. Here's a way to save both time and money: Be deliberate about the errands you run. Plan to visit stores that are close to each other on the same day. Organize your day and week so that you are as efficient as possible, taking care of all of the errands located in one area at the same time. If you commute and have something to take care of in the city you drive to, make sure to do it at lunch or before or after work, so you don't need to make a separate trip in on the weekends. A little extra planning can significantly cut back on your gas consumption.

Store your car, not boxes, in the garage if you have one. (For suggestions on how to get all those boxes out of your garage, see chapter ten on organizing.) This will protect it from inclement weather, wear and tear, and theft.

There's nothing like the new-car smell . . . except the used-car savings.

Buying a reliable make and model of a car that is a year or two old may be one of the smartest purchases you can make. In general, cars lose about 15 to 20 percent of their value each year, and the biggest drop in value is when a new car is driven off the lot. Buying a used car will ensure that you don't pay top sticker price for an asset that will immediately begin to lose value. "A car is a depreciating asset, and I feel that especially when you are young, you should be putting your money into good assets, things that help generate money, as opposed to taking money out of your pocket," says John Brandt of Southern Virginia University.

GROCERIES

Get organized. Go with a list, and stick to it, and get in and out of the store quickly. Don't shop when you are hungry or distracted. Shop as few times per month as possible.

Compare ads for the lowest prices on meat, produce, and items you regularly buy. Shop at stores that will match competitors' ads.

Consider joining a free couponing or shopping service (available through many local newspapers) that will alert you to good grocery deals in your area. You can also sign up for a fee-based service like Deals to Meals, which helps people build a food storage supply and use it. It's available in many Western states. Visit www. dealstomeals.com for more information.

Buy in bulk because single-serving items cost more. Make sure that you can use or freeze everything you buy, however, because it's still money wasted if you have to throw something away. You may want to see if you can split with a friend bulk items that you can't freeze, store, or use.

Store brands can be significantly cheaper than brand-name items. Sometimes generic items are as good as their brand-name counterparts. Other times, it's not worth saving the twenty-five cents for a lower-quality product. Really, the only way to tell is by testing different generic products to see if their quality holds up. We like to buy generic staples such as sugar, flour, rice, and oil and buy name-brand items for things such as frozen pizza, cereal, and deli meat.

Cook from scratch. Prepackaged meals cost a lot more than those you make yourself, and home-cooked meals always taste better than something you defrost.

DINING OUT

Look for coupons in the mail, the newspaper, and on the web for your favorite restaurant, and use them. Remember to bring them to the restaurant and to alert your server when you are ordering that you plan to use a coupon.

Order only appetizers or dessert, or split an entrée. Usually restaurant portions far exceed the number of fat and calories suitable for one person. Skip the drinks and have water instead.

Go to lunch instead of dinner, or dine early enough to take advantage of early bird specials. Some restaurants also offer dining deals on weekdays, so check your favorite restaurant's website for promotions before you plan.

ENTERTAINMENT

If you are a student, take advantage of student discounts offered at some movie theaters, museums, and live theaters. Everyone can go to matinee showings of movie and live theaters for cheaper ticket prices. (For movies, the dollar cinema [if your town has one] is also a great way to have a movie-theater experience for the price of a home rental.) And don't buy food at a movie theater. You can have a nice dinner at a restaurant for the same price you'll pay for soda, popcorn, and candy.

Entertain at home by hosting a game or movie night with your friends. You can further defray the cost by asking everyone to bring an appetizer or a favorite treat to share.

Use your library card to check out DVDs and books. You can also borrow these items from friends. Just be sure to return them in good condition and on time. Natalie had a friend whose overdue book fees snowballed into hundreds of dollars.

Scour the "free events" listings of your local newspaper or city entertainment websites. Universities are a great place to see art, music, and theater for free or for a nominal price. And keep a look out for coupons on city deals websites and in newspapers. Often you can find deep discounts and two-for-one coupons for many entertainment venues, from bowling alleys to miniature golf establishments.

If you have kids, consider trading babysitting nights with another couple so you won't have to pay a babysitter. Some people even form babysitting co-ops that allow them to have several weekends off a month in exchange for a monthly night of babysitting. We've both done this, and it was well worth the effort.

ᘓ CLOTHING AND BEAUTY

Only buy things on sale. Sign up to be on an email list of your favorite store, so you'll be alerted to sales and promotions. Ask around at your favorite store to see if there are certain days when items are usually marked down. It's especially good to buy basic, timeless pieces in off-season clearances. In the early spring, you can often get a nice winter coat, for example, for 50 to 70 percent off its original price. And buy swimsuits for next year in the early fall when these items are deeply discounted. It takes a little bit of self-control to plan that far in advance (who wants to think about snowsuits when the weather is finally starting to warm up?), but it can lead to extreme savings if you do. Natalie keeps a short list in her wallet of items she, her husband, or kids may need, so she can quickly scour sales racks and avoid "they're practically giving it away" purchases that aren't really necessary.

᛫ Invest and spend more money on classic wardrobe basics that you can wear year after year, such as suits, jeans, black pants, white button-down shirts, ties (for men), and one or two really good handbags (women). Buy cheaper trendier items that may only be in style for a season or two. Elyssa likes to pay a little more for designer jeans, which will last for years, but she buys most of her tops at Target.

❧ Do designer looks for less. Stores like Ross and TJMaxx offer designer clothes at discount prices. Also, stores such as Kohl's and Target offer lower-priced lines by high-end designers such as Vera Wang (Kohl's) and Isaac Mizrahi (Target).

❧ Shop consignment, vintage, and thrift stores for beautifully timeless looks at lower prices. Just make sure that the garment fits right and that it can be altered if needed. Don't buy anything that is stained or ripped beyond simple repair.

❧ Try to avoid buying clothes that require dry cleaning, which can rack up a hefty bill. Many men's shirts do not need to be dry-cleaned but can simply be laundered on the gentle cycle and ironed at home.

❧ Trade your old clothes in for cash or trade. Some stores, such as Plato's Closet, will trade gently used brand-name clothing for cash or store credit. For a list of Plato's Closet locations, visit www.platoscloset.com.

❧ Consider hosting a clothing-swap party with your friends. The idea is that all the participants meet a central location and bring items that they no longer fit into or care to wear. Everyone has the opportunity to then go through each other's clothes and take home a "new" wardrobe. (You could do this with home décor or kitchenware too).

❧ Invest in the supplies to give yourself manicures and pedicures at home. And some edible foods make great spa treatments. Chilled cucumbers refresh your eyes, while steamed, mashed strawberries and honey (a handful of strawberries and a tablespoon of honey) make for a delicious skin scrub.

❧ Ask your stylist for a low-maintenance hairstyle. Try a color close to your natural one so that you can go longer in between touch-ups. Avoid fussy haircuts that need frequent updating.

∽ FITNESS

Before you join a gym and commit to a monthly or up-front payment, see what other options are available. Could you run outside? Is there a free track nearby? If you are a student, can you use your school's facilities?

If you have space to store such items, it may be cheaper to invest in a treadmill or stationary bike than to join a gym. You can sometimes find used fitness equipment in good working condition online or in newspaper classifieds.

Save time, money, and the environment by making exercise a part of your daily transportation. Can you walk or bike to work or to do some errands? If so, you'll be exercising without even having to log time at the gym.

Before you invest in a big-ticket item such as, say, a road bicycle, try renting one to see if it's something you will want to use consistently. You can also buy used sporting equipment through classified listings in the newspaper or online, or at a used sporting goods store.

∽ TRAVEL

Do your research. Try visiting Kayak.com, which compares hundreds of travel sites to help you find the best deals.

Travel in the off-season and be flexible. The less rigid your itinerary, the more likely you are to score a great vacation deal.

Consider a "staycation." If you can't afford or don't want to spend the money on leaving town, use your time off from work or school to explore your area's hidden treasures. Maybe there is an artsy town an hour away from you with great museums and antique stores, or perhaps your city has some spectacular hiking trails nearby. City tourism websites are a great place to start researching the things you never knew were so close by.

Book a package. You can sometimes save hundreds of dollars by combining the cost of airfare, hotel, and rental car. Natalie once booked a flight and hotel for a few hundred less than the cost of the flight alone. She didn't need the hotel (and never even checked in), but you can bet she now always searches multiple trip options to make sure she is getting the best deal.

For cheap accommodations, it's hard to beat a tent and a sleeping bag. Low-cost camping trips provide an opportunity to escape to the great outdoors and experience the beauty of Mother Nature. Depending on the campsite you choose, you may have to pay a daily use fee, especially if you are camping in a national park or government-maintained area. But typically those fees are incredibly inexpensive when compared to the cost of a hotel room.

Other ways to save on hotel rooms include booking a hostel or bed and breakfast, or swapping houses with someone by using a web service such as Homexchange.com. You can also use sites such as Priceline.com or Hotwire.com to bid on discount hotels or airfare. Just remember that you have to be a bit adventurous and flexible with sites like these.

SWEET SETUP
Household Essentials

One night when Natalie and her husband, Todd, were engaged, they headed to a superstore to register for wedding gifts. As they walked up and down the aisles, selecting items for their first home, it quickly became clear that neither had a firm idea of what was necessary to run a household—or why they needed it.

Questions bounced back and forth between them as they pondered thread counts and cutlery patterns. The night took a humorous turn on an aisle lined with bath towels. There, Todd suggested registering for two towels—one for him, another for her.

The situation is laughable now, but it begs the question, just what do you really need to set up a house? Knowing what to buy can be overwhelming to say the least. Sifting through aisles upon aisles (and web pages upon web pages) of options in search of the perfect solution is time consuming and usually confusing.

• THE NEWLYWED GAME •

Whether you're setting up a house for the first time or replacing items for the second (or third, or fourth) time, you've likely asked yourself: How many sheet sets do I really need? Is a frittata pan a culinary necessity? Will I ever use a cake stand?

The answer to the above questions, and many more, is a resounding—it depends! Our response may sound wishy-washy, but we like to think of it as empowering. Because at the heart of all these questions is the truth that only you know what you really need.

Buy only what you will use and know how to use—not what you'd like to learn how to use or think you should use. (Think of all the exercise equipment gathering dust in basements everywhere under the premise of, "Once I own it, I'll use it all the time.")

We'll discuss this in more detail in chapter ten but nothing ruins a beautiful home like clutter. Start with the basics you know you need, and then add items as you realize you can't live without them.

After you've mastered the art of the frittata, by all means, splurge on a custom pan. (As long as you can afford it.) With your firsthand knowledge, you'll make a much more informed purchase.

One more caution: Resist the urge to buy something just because it is cheap. We love the thrill of a bargain as much as the next girl in line at Target, but spending for spending's sake is never a great idea. It is usually worth it to spend more on what you truly love and will use, especially when it comes to items as non-disposable as housewares.

We've provided a by-the-room outline of common household items below, with a Latter-day Saint twist. You won't find wine stemware on any list in this guide, but you will find wheat grinders.

Read on, and we'll walk you through the basics. Remember, you needn't buy all of these items at once, and you may find certain ones don't fit your needs.

• Kitchen •

∽ COOKWARE

Gift registry outlines at most national retailers will encourage you to purchase a ten or fourteen-piece set of cookware. Cookware sets are typically well priced and offer a significant savings off the per-item price tag. However, with that savings you lose the luxury of selecting pieces that will really work best for you. So unless you really fall in love with a set, we recommend buying à la carte. That way, you can stock your kitchen with pots and pans made from different metals and finishes, just like a professional kitchen.

Common metals are copper, aluminum, anodized aluminum, stainless steel, and cast iron. Copper conducts heat beautifully but requires polishing and is quite pricey. Aluminum conducts heat quickly and evenly, and is usually combined with another metal, hence anodized aluminum. Stainless steel is durable and beautiful but doesn't conduct heat quite as quickly as other metals, so it is usually combined with a more conductive metal. Cast iron takes a while to heat up, but once it does, it holds heat evenly for a long time.

Surface finishes include nonstick, stick resistant, and porcelain enamel. Non-stick cookware is great for cooking without oil. Cleanup is usually a breeze too. However, gourmands prefer stainless-steel pans because they are better for searing, deglazing, and extracting better flavor from food.

Here are a few cookware recommendations from Todd Leonard, a chef and assistant professor at Utah Valley University's Culinary Arts Institute.[1]

- stainless-steel pots with double-insulated bottoms to better conduct heat
- straight-sided sauté pan
- sloped-sided sauté pan
- rondeau (also called a braiser, it's a circular-type roasting pan)

- two-gallon stockpot
- three-gallon stockpot
- two-quart sauce pan
- three-quart sauce pan
- one small or medium nonstick pan
- one large nonstick pan
- Dutch oven
- cast-iron skillet

⌐ SPOONS AND TOOLS

If you buy nonstick cookware, make sure you also purchase nonstick utensils, which won't scratch the surface. (Elyssa learned the hard way that a nonstick pan is ruined when you scrape it with a metal spoon.) Keep all metals away from nonstick surfaces. Tell everyone in the house not to use them, either. The following are our recommendations for kitchen tools.

- perforated spoon
- wooden spoons
- whisks (heavy-duty and "balloon")
- tongs
- spatulas
- baster
- meat thermometer
- candy thermometer
- frying thermometer (for measuring oil temperature)
- juicer
- grater

- microplane
- vegetable peeler
- garlic press
- ice cream scoop
- rolling pin
- pastry blender
- cookie cutters
- colander to strain large items
- chinois (a cone-shaped, fine mesh sieve used for sauces)
- cutting boards (We're sticklers about cross-contamination and use color-coded cutting boards for different functions.)
- spice rack
- salad spinner

BAKEWARE

Plastic, glass, stainless steel, melamine, rubber—there is no shortage of options when it comes to selecting bakeware and baking tools. Our best recommendation when selecting these items is to work backward. Look at your end product and

think about what would make it (or the process) better. A nonstick surface that would more easily release cupcakes? A mixing bowl with a pour spout for less countertop splatters? Or a larger bread pan for bigger bread? Here is a place to start:

- stainless-steel or plastic measuring cups
- two-cup glass measuring cup
- eight-cup glass measuring bowl

- ❧ measuring spoons
- ❧ stainless-steel bowls for mixing
- ❧ plastic bowls
- ❧ half-sheet pans (several)
- ❧ rectangular cake pan
- ❧ two cupcake pans
- ❧ two round cake pans (for double-layer cakes)
- ❧ Bundt cake pan (or angel food cake pan)
- ❧ springform pan (or specialty cheesecake pan)
- ❧ loaf pans for bread (pick a size that you like best)
- ❧ casserole dishes (9-by-13 glass dishes)
- ❧ cooling racks
- ❧ jars or canisters to hold baking basics such as sugar and flour
- ❧ pizza stone

❧ CUTLERY

Good knives make it easier and faster to cook and help prevent injuries. (A dull knife is often more dangerous than a sharp one).

There are different styles of knives, such as Western and Eastern. Blades are made from a handful of metals, including stainless steel or high-carbon stainless steel. Stainless-steel blades are resistant to rust and stains. High-carbon stainless steel offers hard blades with the aforementioned qualities.

Knives are made with several manufacturing techniques. The most desirable is full tang, which means that metal runs the length of the knife handle. Chapter four has a detailed discussion on knives and knife safety.

Chef Todd Leonard says every kitchen should have at least these four basics:

- ❧ chef's knife (between 8 and 12 inches)

29

- sharpening steel
- paring knife
- boning knife

As you can afford, add:

- Santoku knife (a Japanese-style knife good for chopping vegetables)
- cleavers
- bread knife with serrated edge
- slicing knife
- filet knife
- kitchen shears
- pliers for fish
- melon baller
- apple-corer
- Tourne knife (a paring knife with a curved blade)

SMALL APPLIANCES

Small appliances seem, well, small, but once you've got a handful of them, they actually command a large chunk of cabinet space. We like to keep only frequently used items on the countertop, with the rest relegated to a pantry or cabinet. It helps keep our kitchens organized and uncluttered.

When selecting appliances, it may be helpful to look at what you saw your parents use in the kitchen. If your dad cooked pancakes on a large griddle every Saturday, you'll probably instinctively want one too.

- toaster or toaster oven
- waffle iron
- blender

- ✧ griddle
- ✧ slow cooker
- ✧ rice cooker
- ✧ stand mixer
- ✧ wheat grinder
- ✧ juicer
- ✧ food processor
- ✧ ice cream maker
- ✧ bread machine
- ✧ very small electric appliances: can opener, knife, kettle, immersion blender

ᶜ A NOTE ON WHEAT GRINDERS

If you're going to store wheat in your long-term food storage (see chapter six), you really need at least a hand-crank wheat grinder. Basic versions are available online at Amazon.com and at retailers nationwide, including Walmart. They cost around sixty dollars.

Those who grind and use wheat frequently need both a hand-crank mill (for electricity-free milling) and an electric mill. (Or a portable generator powerful enough to run the mill when the electricity's out!) There are lots of reputable electric grain mills on the market, ranging in price from one hundred fifty to four hundred dollars.

ᶜ DINNERWARE

Most dinnerware is sold either as a set (of, say, four or eight place settings) or as separate pieces. Fine china is often sold per place setting; one place setting equals one person. As with the cookware, assess your needs before purchasing a large set. It may come with items you won't use frequently or at all, like teacups and saucers. (Then again, those could come in handy for faux tea parties).

If you plan on entertaining at all, you'll likely want enough matching dinnerware to feed twelve people. You could also purchase six settings from two patterns for a mix-and-match look.

There are many kinds of dinnerware, including fine china, stoneware, and everyday dinnerware like Corelle. If you'll use fine china for fancy dinners a few times a year—and have somewhere to store all those extra plates and bowls—it is a nice tradition to embrace. But don't feel guilty if china just isn't your thing.

"Keep it basic and classic," says Caitlin Creer, a Salt Lake City interior decorator. "White works with any holiday. You can add napkins and other accessories to dress it up. Silver sandstone is pretty too. Polka dot plates are cute, but you probably won't want those as your main dishes for years."[2]

The essentials include:

- ❧ soup bowls
- ❧ cereal bowls
- ❧ pasta bowls
- ❧ salad plates
- ❧ dinner plates
- ❧ dessert dishes

∽ GLASSWARE

Don't overspend on glassware—especially if you have kids or plan to—because you'll likely be replacing them soon. (Natalie bought inexpensive plastic cups and plates for her kids to use, but it seems like glasses still break every few weeks. Elyssa doesn't even get mad about broken glasses anymore. She just sighs and tells her kids—or her husband—to remember to use their assigned plastic ones.)

Look for a classic shape that will be comfortable to drink from. Pick up a glass to check for weight: Does it feel heavy or just right? Check to see if you can grip your hand around the entire glass, so it is stable in your hand. Also, make sure it holds enough liquid.

You'll probably want:

- ⚜ glasses, tall and short
- ⚜ juice glasses
- ⚜ mugs
- ⚜ glass goblets (for mocktails and other fancy drinks)

⚘ SERVEWARE

There is something to be said for serving dinner straight from a pot on the stove—buffet style, if you will. Fewer dishes being dirtied and no searching for hot pads.

But if company is coming, and soup from a pot on the stove isn't quite appealing, serveware comes in handy. This includes larger (and perhaps fancier) spoons, forks, and ladles for dishing up. Salad tongs are the best for grabbing your greens. Nicer glass or ceramic bowls are handy for side dishes or rolls, and platters work great for appetizers or desserts. Save time and money by purchasing oven-safe casserole or cake dishes that look good going from the oven to table.

You'll probably need:

- ⚜ medium platter
- ⚜ large platter
- ⚜ gravy boat
- ⚜ salt and pepper shakers

- pitchers
- cake stand and cover (to keep cake from drying out)
- serving utensils

LINENS AND THINGS

For cleaning and serving, it is a good idea to stock the following:

- flour-sack dish towels, for covering baked goods that need to rise
- absorbent terrycloth dish towels, for drying dishes
- old or stained dish towels, for cleaning up spills
- kitchen rags
- oven mitts
- pot holders
- napkins and napkin rings
- place mats
- tablecloths

EXTRA, EXTRA

There are other accessories you can buy to pretty up your kitchen and make it more functional. However, these things, like cookbook holders, spoon rests, or paper towel dispensers, definitely aren't necessities, so purchase those as you (and your budget) see fit.

• BATHROOM •

Convention advises stocking three towels per person: one for current use, one on the shelf, and one in the laundry. Depending on how often you do the laundry, and how judicious you are in hanging towels to dry, you could probably sneak by with two per person.

The trick with towels is to buy them thick enough that they absorb enough water but not so thick that they never dry. (Natalie's maternal grandmother calls the latter "thick and thirsty" towels.) Cotton or cotton blends are used for most towels. High-quality cotton is based on fiber lengths. Longer fibers create more luxurious, strong, and absorbent cotton. There are many common types of cotton, like Egyptian, Pima, Supima, and Turkish, each noted for different qualities.

In each bathroom, we recommend:

- bath towels or bath sheets (bath towels are standard size, while sheets are wraparound large)
- hand towels
- washcloths
- bath mat
- shower curtain and liner
- shower curtain rod and rings
- soap dish (or dispenser, depending on what you prefer)
- toothbrush holder
- wastebasket

• BEDROOM •

When it comes to selecting sheets, thread count is often king. Simply put, the thread count is the number of threads per square inch of fabric. Higher thread counts are indicative of a softer, more durable product. (Top-of-the-line sheets are pricey, but good-quality sheets can be found in many price ranges).

Bed sheets are typically made of cotton or a cotton/polyester blend. All-cotton is preferred over a blend because it is softer and more breathable. However,

100 percent cotton will wrinkle more than polyester.

Sheets are also offered in different weaves, like sateen or pinpoint or flannel. Choose what touch feels best to you. If you live in a colder climate, it may be nice to have a set of cozy flannel sheets on hand for winter months.

Make sure you purchase the right size. Most fitted sheets come in standard, pillow top, or extra-deep varieties.

For each bed, consider:

- fitted sheets
- flat sheets
- bed skirt
- pillows: natural fill, down, synthetic, or memory foam
- pillow protectors
- pillowcases
- mattress pad
- mattress protector
- comforter (or duvet and duvet cover)
- blanket or coverlet

· LAUNDRY ROOM ·

Closet or castle, there are a few things almost every laundry room needs. You'll likely want to store cleaning items on this list in a broom closet near your kitchen and extra supplies in your laundry space.

- washing machine
- dryer
- vacuum
- mop and broom

- ✧ trash can
- ✧ iron
- ✧ ironing board and cover
- ✧ clothes hanging rack
- ✧ cleaning caddy

• HOME MAINTENANCE •

Even if DIY isn't your thing, you'll need at least these tools around to do basic maintenance:

- ✧ hammer
- ✧ screwdrivers: Phillips and flat-head
- ✧ crescent wrench
- ✧ level
- ✧ tape measure
- ✧ cordless drill
- ✧ rubber mallet (indispensable when assembling from-a-box furniture)

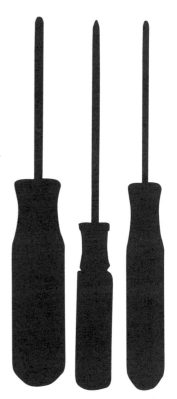

PERFECTLY PLANNED
Menu Forecasting
& Grocery Shopping

The question "What's for dinner?" can be a challenge or a nightmare, depending on when you ask it. If you are deciding what to fix for dinner at, well, dinnertime, you'll probably be stuck with a frozen pizza, drive-thru hamburgers, or a tub of frosting and stale graham crackers (Elyssa's favorite!).

Food is a huge spending category for any individual or family. And while it's not a category you can eliminate altogether, it's definitely one you can manage. Here are a few ways to do it.

• EAT AT HOME •

This is perhaps the most dramatic and effective way to trim your food budget. Now, understand that we're not asking you to give up eating out altogether. Eating out can serve important social purposes, and, honestly, sometimes it is just so nice to eat a fancy, complicated meal without having to worry about the cleanup afterward.

The important thing about eating out, however, is that it's a planned outing meant as a treat and reward—and not an act of desperation. No more going to the drive-thru because you are hungry, or because you saw a mouthwatering ad for the triple-bacon cheeseburger on TV. As you plan your month, it's important to pencil in a few meals out as a reward for mostly cooking and eating at home. But they should be the exception to the rule.

One other great thing about cooking at home is the dramatic health benefits you'll reap. Fast food and restaurant food typically have overblown portion sizes and are high in salt, fat, and calories. At home, you can control your caloric intake and maximize the nutrients you consume.

• PLAN IT OUT •

Without question eating at home will save you money, but there are things you can do to further reduce your food bill. Menu forecasting and smart grocery shopping will save you buckets of money—and time.

We've found it is most helpful to plan out a week's worth of meals at a time. Some people like to plan for two weeks or for an entire month, but planning week to week allows for both consistency and flexibility. As you become more organized and stock your pantry with food, you may find that you can go to the grocery store even less. And that's a great thing. The fewer times you go to the grocery store, the more money you can save.

What you eat in a given week should depend on three things: your schedule, what needs to be used up in your fridge, and what's on sale. Before you sit down to plan the week's menu, take a look at what's going on. Do you have a dance concert or a church activity one evening? Are there some days you will have little or no time to cook? Is there someone you need to bring a meal to? Looking over your week will allow you to assign simple meals or leftovers to busy days and more complicated fare to days when you have extra time.

Next, go through your refrigerator and see what's about to go bad. Food thrown away amounts to dollars wasted, so if you have produce that's rapidly

ripening or buttermilk that's nearing the expiration date, plan your menus to incorporate those items. Some websites, such as Allrecipes.com and Supercook .com, even allow you to build meals around specific ingredients.

These types of sites can be a valuable resource. Using leftovers will be discussed in more detail in chapter four.

The third thing you need to consider is what is on sale. You always want to purchase food at the lowest price possible (more on that later), so if you can get a great price on chicken and avocados, it might be just the week for fajitas.

"If you are watching the sales and planning your menus around them, that is where you can save a lot of money," said Shandra Madsen,[1] owner of Deals to Meals, a Utah-based service that helps people build their food storage and use it. Her website tells readers what items to stock up on each week by comparing the sales at major grocery stores to discount retailers like Walmart and warehouse stores such as Sam's Club and Costco. For a small monthly fee, readers have access to the website and its sale information. It is available in a dozen western states at www.dealstomeals.com.

Another way to find sales is to compare advertisements yourself. Most grocery stores produce print ad circulars saying what they have on sale for the week. It may vary by area, but most store sales run midweek to midweek (for example, a Wednesday to the following Tuesday). These ads can be found at the store and often in the newspaper or in your mailbox, depending on the store and your area. Check with your favorite store to see how management distributes its advertisements, and be sure to look online. Some stores, such as Walmart, will match all of their competitors' printed prices for identical items. We prefer to shop at these kinds of stores, so we can take advantage of sales throughout the city but only make one trip.

• STRATEGIZE WAYS TO • BUILD YOUR PANTRY

If you go through the circulars yourself, watch for items that you regularly buy to go on sale, and watch for nonperishable items to hit rock-bottom prices. (The more you compare ads, the more you'll be able to tell when something is a really good price. A subscription service like Deals to Meals will do the work for you.) You never want to pay full price for one can of beans, let alone twenty, so when you find a killer deal, it's time to pounce. In fact, consider buying as close to a year's supply as you can afford, recommends Madsen of Deals to Meals. This may mean you initially spend more money up front, but over time it will save you hundreds of dollars each year. You always want to buy food at its lowest price. If you can buy sixteen cans of peanut butter when it's a dollar, Madsen says, then you won't have to run to the store and pay full price for it at $3.49.

If you're searching the ads yourself, be sure to circle items you plan to purchase in a way that stands out, and take note of the unit size. (For example, a sixteen-ounce bottle of juice may be on sale, whereas a twenty-ounce bottle is still full price. To get the sale, you'll need to choose the right size.) If you intend to price match, have all of the ads organized, and be sure to bring them to the store with you.

Should you use coupons? There are countless books and websites devoted to couponing, and some people make a career of it. Coupons definitely have a place, but only for items you will actually use. It's a good idea to go through the coupons in the newspaper (or those you receive via direct mail) and pull out any for items you know you want to purchase. If there is a particular brand you like, you can visit the company's website to look for deals and promotions. In general, the best way to use coupons is to combine them with store promotions for bonus savings. Just remember to keep them organized and to only use them for things you need. It doesn't matter if you get a killer deal on shampoo if you hate the brand and have no intention of ever using it. Shop smart.

• WRITE OUT YOUR MENUS •

Once you have figured out what you can buy on sale, it's time to plan the menu for the week. Every good menu plan should deliberately include leftovers. This eliminates waste, saves money, and saves time. Planning leftovers doesn't mean you have to eat tacos three nights in a row. But, if you can get a great price on lean ground beef, buy two and a half pounds instead of one and use it twice during the week. Brown all the ground beef the first night. Use half for tacos and set the other half aside for shepherd's pie two days later. (Be sure to use it by the use-by date on the package.) If chicken is on sale, cook it all in a slow cooker at the beginning of the week. Reserve some for enchiladas or a casserole in the beginning of the week, and freeze some for soup a few days later.

It's also important to consider what's in season when you plan your week's meals. It's maddening that you can get all kinds of high-calorie junk food for less than two dollars, but good luck finding a carton of blueberries for that price most of the year. Fresh fruits and vegetables are expensive, but they are a crucial part of any diet. The best way to reduce the cost of produce is to buy in season. This means loading up on watermelon in the summer and apples in the fall. Cook hearty soups with winter squashes in December and January, and enjoy fruit salads in the summer. You can supplement your produce needs with canned and frozen fruits and vegetables, but there is nothing like fresh fruits and vegetables eaten at their peak.

• MAKE A LIST •

Grocery shopping without a list is just asking for trouble. Once you have planned your meals for the week, you need to make a list of all the ingredients you will need to cook those meals, as well as a list of other items you regularly keep on hand (bread, milk, fruits, vegetables, and so on). And remember that you need everything a recipe calls for, so you may need to buy condiments or spices, depending on what you already have.

It's easiest and most efficient to make your list in an order that follows the layout of the grocery store. List all your produce in one section, all your meats in another, and all your dairy yet another. This will save you time so you aren't wandering from one aisle to another looking for list items. (Natalie's highly organized and fabulous mother-in-law keeps printouts of her grocery store list on a clipboard. The list includes common items and space for not-so-common ones. All she has to do is put check marks by what she needs and she is good to go.)

Once you've made the list, make sure that it actually makes it to the store. (It's comical how many times we've forgotten ours.) And be sure to bring any ad circulars or coupons you plan to use.

· GET IN AND GET OUT · AT THE GROCERY STORE

To save money at the store, you need to stick to your list and hustle through the store. Ever been to the store to buy ice cream and come home with a cart full of unplanned purchases? Who knew that nail polish was going to be on sale, or that you favorite celebrity was going to be on the cover of a gossip magazine? The longer you stay in a store, the more money you are likely to spend. Sure, you need to take the time to make sure you are selecting the right things, but there shouldn't be any time to linger.

You also need to be wary of the distractions and triggers that can cause you to spend extra money. Here are a few tips:

- ❁ Bring a list and stick to it.
- ❁ Eat before you go. Nothing can cause you to overbuy as much as hunger.

- ❧ Pick a consistent time to shop when you won't be tired or overly stressed.

- ❧ If you have them, leave the kids (and spouse) at home. Even if you have to hire a babysitter, the five dollars or so an hour it will cost is nothing compared to additional toys and on-the-spot-snacks you'll have to buy to keep them from shrieking (spouses included!).

- ❧ Don't shop and talk on your cell phone. Distracted shopping often leads to unwise purchases.

- ❧ Put away in the blink of an eye

Here's a quick tip: Just as you organize your grocery list, try and organize items as you shop and then group them together on the conveyer belt so you or the clerk can put them in bags in an organized fashion. For instance, keep produce together, canned items together, and so forth. (It's helpful to leave out any items you intend to price match until the very end. Then you can quickly run through the sale-match items with your clerk. Again, it's fastest to have the competitor's ads out and ready to show the person who is ringing you up. To further expedite checking out, hold back any items for which you have coupons until the end.)

To save time when you return home from the grocery store, take all of the items out of the grocery bags before you put them away. This will allow you to visually assess everything that you purchased so that you can put more like items away at a time. For instance, if you can see all of the items that go in the freezer, you will hopefully only have to open it a few times. Same goes for the items that need to be put in the pantry, cold storage, and the refrigerator.

And remember to place things neatly in their correct locations, where you can best see them so you'll be quickly reminded of what you have bought. If you aren't planning to cook all your meat at once, or if there is anything else you need to freeze, put the appropriate portions in the freezer, labeled with a date. As you go through the week, try to consume perishable items such as produce early in the week when they are at their freshest. (For more tips on freezing food, see chapter seven on gardening and food preservation.)

WHATCHA GOT COOKIN'?

One of the coolest things about cooking is it's a skill you will likely practice on some level every day of your life. Everyone has to eat. Think: if you played the piano every day, or worked on woodcarving or sewed elaborate quilts, you'd probably be pretty good, right? Well, with cooking you get to practice pretty much anytime you need to eat. The other cool thing about cooking is that, when you start to do it well, there is a tasty reward at the end for your efforts.

Kitchen catastrophes—a lot of them, actually—are bound to happen along the way. Keep your sense of humor and a frozen pizza on hand and enjoy the learning process for what it is.

• GETTING STARTED •
COOK WHAT YOU LIKE AND KNOW

This is a bit of a no-brainer, but start by making the foods you like to eat. It will be that much more motivating if you are working with ingredients you already enjoy. If you like Chinese food, for example, invest in a Chinese cookbook, start at the beginning, and cook your way to the end. Also, it's important to be true to your heritage and the foods you grew up with, says Todd Leonard,[1] a chef instructor/assistant professor at Utah Valley University's Culinary Arts Institute. (He is also an executive chef over product development at the Utah-based company Shelf Reliance.) Chef Todd, as he's known, says to cook what's familiar. You've probably tasted great fried chicken, or a great pasta dish, or maybe your mom makes a killer lasagna. Because you already have exposure to these foods, you know what they should look and taste like. So start simple and save the exotic dishes for later. "Master the things you know, and do those things well, and then expand your horizons," says Chef Todd.

Although cooking classes will certainly build your skill set and increase your confidence, you don't need any sort of formal fancy training to be a good cook. You just need to get started, learning through trial and error as you follow recipes. When you are learning to cook, it's best to start with recipes with only a few ingredients and steps. These will build your confidence and teach you fundamentals that will prepare you for more complicated fare. And, as a beginner, follow the recipes exactly. As you start to understand the ways foods work together, you can adapt recipes to your own liking. But, for now, stick to the suggested ingredients and cooking methods.

· WHERE TO FIND RECIPES ·

Just ask: One of the best ways to tell if a recipe is good is to try it. Working backward from that principle, anytime you eat a food you like at a friend's house, neighborhood barbecue, or work party, ask for the recipe. Latter-day Saint wards can be a particularly great source for recipes. If you like a stew served at a week-day Relief Society meeting, or a dip served at a ward activity, by all means ask for the recipe. Chances are, whoever brought the dish will be extremely flattered.

Consider the cookbook. Blogger Julie Powell taught herself to cook elaborate French dishes by cooking her way through Julia Child's dense *Mastering the Art of French Cooking: Volume 1* (Alfred A. Knopf) one dish at a time. She later wrote about her efforts in the national bestseller *Julie & Julia*, which became a movie starring Meryl Streep and Amy Adams. All that from cooking through a cookbook! While Julia Child's cookbook isn't for beginners, you could do the same exercise by cooking your way through a basic cookbook like the *Betty Crocker Cookbook New Edition*, published in 2005.

Use the Internet. The web is a wonderful place to find recipes because of its search functionality. Sites such as Allrecipes.com allow you to search for recipes by name or ingredient. (We find it helpful to type the word *easy* into the site's search field.) For more advanced chefs, the Food Network has an impressive, searchable site, and sites like Epicurious.com will surely inspire your inner foodie. And Elyssa and Natalie are both obsessed with finding and storing recipes on the website Pinterest.com. You can search the online bulletin board for any dish you heart desires and then "pin" it to your own account for easy access. If you don't already have a Pinterest account, we highly recommend getting one. You'll be amazed at the inspiration available for virtually every area of homemaking.

Borrow from bloggers. There are a lot of fantastic amateur (and professional!) chefs out there making good food and blogging about it. These blogs often have pictures and detailed recipes that you can try at home.

Turn on your TV. Shows on the Food Network and other cooking programs will not only provide recipes, but they will also provide a wealth of food education, demonstrating some dishes step by step so you can watch and learn. For example, Natalie learned how to properly chop an onion by watching the Food Network.

• TOOLS OF THE TRADE •

For many years, Elyssa got by in the kitchen with only a handful of pans and a set of knives she and her husband received as a wedding gift. That's certainly not the ideal way to start out, but you also don't need a posh, fully stocked kitchen to be a good cook. The best thing to do is to use what you have and acquire quality items bit by bit, amassing useful kitchen supplies as you go. (You can always hint to friends and family that kitchen items make great gifts.)

Here are a few tips on pots and pans as recommended by Chef Todd of Utah Valley University. Note that his suggestions for a well-stocked kitchen are also listed in chapter two, and that knives will be discussed later in the chapter.

When purchasing pots, Chef Todd recommends you only buy ones that are stainless steel. You also want to make sure that they are double-insulated on the bottom, which helps to better conduct heat as you are cooking. It's handy to have both two- and three-gallon stock pots so that you can use the one most appropriate for the size of stew or soup you are making. You'll also need sauté pans, saucepans, and nonstick pans, so that you can cook everything from butter and vegetables (sauté pan) to eggs and pancakes (nonstick). Chef Todd recommends having a straight-sided and a slope-sided sauté pan (called a sauteuse in French), and having two- and three-quart saucepans. When you can, buy a small or medium nonstick pan and a large one. It's also nice to have a rondeau (a circular type of roasting pan also called a braiser), a cast-iron skillet, a Dutch oven, and a slow cooker (discussed later). And for ease and convenience in the kitchen, you can't beat a KitchenAid or other type of stand mixer and a food processor.

Remember that it's not necessary to acquire everything at once. Even if all you have is a couple of pots and pans and a cute apron, those items will at least get you started.

• BEFORE YOU BURN IT, •
THINK AND LISTEN

"Most of cooking is common sense," says Chef Todd Leonard. "What are you doing to the product? Are you just massacring it, or are you giving it its ultimate opportunity?" Becoming a good cook means analyzing a dish and figuring out how to best prepare it. For example, if you are grilling, understand that this is a dry-heat method that works better with fattier meats that are well marbled and can withstand high heat. If you are cooking a hot dog, says Leonard, don't just plop it on the grill on high heat. Instead, slow roast it to give it time to plump and to reach its juiciest, most delicious state.

As you study particular foods you are interested in (using books, the Internet, and TV as your guides), and as you practice, you'll have a better sense of what mastering a dish means. Slow down and really think about what you are doing in the kitchen, suggests Leonard, and also "listen" to your food. If, for example, a chicken in a pan refuses to caramelize, try turning the heat up a bit.

Part of thinking about your food starts with menu forecasting. Any good cook plans his or her weekly menus to purposely include leftovers, says Leonard. "Consider your leftovers a blessing," he says. "Don't be afraid of leftovers; leftovers are our friends." Even if you find you love to spend hours in the kitchen, you still want spend your time there as efficiently as possible. So there is no reason to cook ground beef two nights in a row. If you know that you are going to be using more than one recipe that calls for hamburger meat, cook all of it in one night and save what you don't use in your first meal for later. (If it's going to be more than a day or two, you'll need to freeze the meat.) When Chef Todd makes a béchamel sauce (a simple white sauce) to serve his kids with toast for breakfast, for example, he saves some for later to make macaroni and cheese. Leftovers both eliminate waste and save time.

Also, regularly go through your fridge to see what needs to be used up. That should give you a clue as to what to make for dinner. (Elyssa once took a cooking class where a participant explained that she cooked "Must Go" for dinner, meaning everything in the fridge "must go.") If you've got grapes and apples that are starting to brown, serve up a simple fruit salad as a side dish at dinner. Also when planning your menus, think about what is in season to catch fruits and vegetables at their freshest, most flavorful, and cheapest point. The Fruits & Veggies—More Matters public health campaign has a list of seasonal produce at its website www.fruitsandveggiesmorematters.org.

• PREPARE BY PUTTING THINGS • IN THEIR PLACES

One of the great secrets to enjoying cooking is the concept of *mise en place*. In French, it means "setting in place." In English, we use it to mean having everything in place, ready to be cooked before you actually begin cooking. Before you start throwing things in a pan, you need all of your ingredients prepped and ready. If you are making stir-fry, the vegetables and meat need to be chopped, and the sauce needs to be measured and prepared. That way, you aren't trying to take care of some ingredients when others are burning on the stove. "If you have everything ready, you can go stand at the stove and actually cook and have some fun," says Chef Todd.

It's also important to clean and put away as you go. This keeps your work environment sanitary, and it makes clean up really easy. (You won't have a mountain of dishes and ingredients to deal with at the end.)

• GET COOKING (LITERALLY) •

There are two basic ways to cook things: dry heat and moist heat. Some basic dry-heat methods are baking, broiling, grilling, frying and deep-frying, roasting, and sautéing. Moist heat methods include boiling, braising, poaching, simmering, slow cooking, and steaming. Let's examine each method more closely:

⤿ DRY-HEAT METHODS

⧂ BAKE: To cook food in an oven with dry heat. Covering an item will help it retain its natural moisture, while baking an item uncovered leads to a crisp top.

⧂ BROIL: To cook food directly under a heat source, using high heat. Note that the top of foods will cook very quickly.

⧂ GRILL: To prepare food using a high heat source on a grill. Grills typically use gas or charcoal to heat food.

⧂ FRY: To cook food over moderate to high heat, using fat. When you deep-fry, you use enough hot fat so that the food can float.

⧂ ROAST: To cook meat in an oven on a rack, using a shallow pan. No liquid is added.

⧂ SAUTÉ: To quickly cook food in a small amount of fat in a skillet. The pan should be hot enough so that the food is literally jumping.

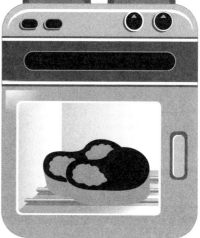

⧂ SEAR: To cook the surface of a food (usually meat) at a high temperature to pull out the juices, which are then caramelized to create a crust.

⧂ STIR-FRY: To cook chopped food in a small amount of fat over high heat, stirring constantly. This method of cooking is popular in many Asian countries.

⌇ MOIST-HEAT METHODS

BOIL: To cook food in water that is boiling, with bubbles rising to the surface and breaking. A rolling boil is one that is so rapid you can't stir the bubbles down.

BRAISE: To cook food for a long time at a low temperature in order to make foods tender and flavorful. Food is first browned in fat, and then cooked at low heat with a tiny amount of juice for several hours. Food should be cooked in a container with a tight-fitting lid to keep the juices from evaporating.

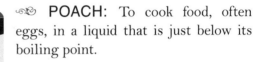

POACH: To cook food, often eggs, in a liquid that is just below its boiling point.

SIMMER: To cook a liquid just below its boiling point, where tiny bubbles just begin to appear.

SLOW COOK: To cook using constant moist heat at a low temperature. This is typically done in a slow cooker. One brand name for a slow cooker is a Crock-Pot. You don't need a Crock-Pot, however, to slow cook something. Many heat sources, particularly the oven, will work fine at a low enough temperature, and for a long enough time.

STEAM: To cook food using steam. This can be done using a rack or steaming basket over boiling water, or it can be done in the microwave with specially manufactured steaming bags.

What method you use for cooking largely depends on the product you are using, says Chef Todd Leonard, and this is when it's important to really think in the kitchen. Ask yourself, "How will this product be best prepared?" As mentioned above, marbled, fatty meat can withstand high heat and works well on the grill. On the other hand, lean, tough meat such as brisket needs to be slow cooked with moisture over low heat to reach its most tender and flavorful potential.

• KNOW YOUR KNIVES •

A knife is one of the most important tools in the kitchen. At a minimum, here are the basic knives you need in the kitchen, according to Chef Todd Leonard: a regular chef's knife between eight and twelve inches long, a paring knife, a boning knife. You will also need a sharpening steel. From there, you could add things such as a Santoku knife (a Japanese-style knife good for chopping vegetables), a filet knife, a bread knife with serrated edges, a meat cleaver, kitchen shears, pliers for fish, a melon baller, and an apple corer.

A sharp knife is both more effective and safer than a dull knife, and it is important to sharpen it with sharpening steel regularly as needed—probably before each meal. Every six months to a year, sharpen your knives on a whetstone or have them professionally sharpened, says Leonard.

To extend the life of your knives, do not wash them in a commercial dishwasher. Always wash and dry them by hand. Put them away promptly. Do not allow knives to sit wet or in water for any length of time. You do not want them to rust.

↪ KNIFE SAFETY

You probably like your fingers, so to make sure you hang on to all ten, here are a few quick knife safety tips from Chef Todd:

- Always cut on a cutting board using the correct knife for the job. To keep the cutting board from slipping around, place a damp towel underneath it.

- Make sure your knife is properly sharpened. (Again, a dull knife is much more dangerous than a sharp one.)

- Always cut away from yourself.

- If you need to walk with a knife, hold it pointed down and close to your leg. Do not try to catch a falling knife. Simply back away and let it fall.

❧ Don't leave knives in a sink of water, where someone could reach in unknowingly and cut him- or herself. Wash them, dry them, and promptly put them away after use.

↶ KNIFE CONTROL

To maximize your time in the kitchen, you want the most efficient tools possible. Do not cut with dull knife; it's frustrating and unsafe. Make sure your knife is sharpened properly, and that you have selected the right knife for the job. Keep the blade's sharp edge on the cutting board, says Todd Leonard, holding the item being cut with three fingertips and your thumb. Use even strokes and a grip on the knife that is most comfortable for you.

Cutting terms:

- **CHOP**: To cut food into bite-size pieces when it's not necessary to have uniformity.

- **DICE**: To cut food into tiny cubes, typically smaller than ½ inch.

- **JULIENNE**: To cut into very thin, match-like strips.

- **MINCE**: To cut food into very small pieces, smaller than when you would chop.

- **SLICE**: To cut into flat pieces.

• SPICE UP YOUR LIFE •

Seasonings such as herbs and spices can take any dish from bland and ordinary to extraordinary, even if you are only adding salt and pepper. Remember that you want to use the highest-quality seasonings you can find. We prefer fresh ground pepper and kosher or sea salt to table salt and pepper. It really does make a difference in flavor.

You can purchase dried herbs (aromatic leaves of certain plants) or purchase or

grow fresh ones. Dried herbs are convenient and inexpensive, but nothing beats fresh herbs for cooking, says Chef Todd. (It would be fantastic to grow, say, basil, oregano, or cilantro in a garden. For gardening advice, see chapter seven.) You can store fresh herbs in the refrigerator for up to two weeks.

Spices come from the seeds, buds, bark, flowers, or roots of plants. Some common spices include allspice, anise, cayenne pepper, cinnamon, cumin, curry, ginger, nutmeg, paprika, saffron, and turmeric. If possible, grind your own spices just before using them for maximum flavor, says Chef Todd. And make sure to store your dried spices in a cool, dark place.

• TRIED-AND-TRUE TIPS •

Here are some additional tips for being a culinary rock star, courtesy of Chef Todd Leonard:

- Use the best ingredients you can find and afford. Find foods in season and when possible, from local growers or farmers' markets. Use beef graded USDA Prime. The better the initial ingredients, the better the finished product.

- Watch how things are measured. For example, one cup of brown sugar is different than one cup of packed brown sugar. A scant measurement, for example a scant teaspoon, means "not quite whole." A heaping measurement, such as a heaping teaspoon, means overflowing. Remember that liquids and dry foods are measured differently as well.

- Embrace (a little) fat. A bit of high-quality butter or olive oil will make all the difference in a dish. Forget the margarine, already!

- Go for cleaner flavor. It may take some extra time, but you'll be glad you skimmed extra grease off of soups, stews, and sauces.

- Stock up on flavor. Substitute stock (a liquid made by simmering bones or vegetables to extract their flavor) for water in everything from sauces to pasta. It's nice to make your own stock, but you can also buy it in the soup aisle of the grocery store. Look for low-sodium versions.

- Don't overcook. Check an item for doneness long before the set recipe time. You can always cook something longer, but once it's burned, you're toast (so to speak). You may also want to check your oven's temperature with an oven thermometer to see how its temperature compares to the set gauges.

• KNOW YOUR MEATS •

Meat will likely be the most expensive part of your meal, so it's crucial you get it right. Elyssa was a vegetarian for most of her teen years and still favors vegetarian dishes, but because she doesn't have the discipline to live a rigorously healthy vegetarian lifestyle, she looks to meat for the necessary protein and iron it provides. Still, the sight of raw chicken breasts or ground hamburger sometimes makes her want to cry, or at least gag a little. You may have a similar response, but the more you work with meat, the more you'll appreciate the versatility and flavor it brings to a meal. When cooking meat, it's especially important to be a fanatic about cleanliness and follow the recommended food safety guidelines (discussed at length later).

ANATOMY OF A COW

Don't know a shank from a sirloin? Don't worry. It's fair to say that most people don't. But understanding different cuts of meat will help you know what to purchase at the grocery store and how to prepare it later. Because beef comes in a great variety of cuts, we'll discuss it here as an overall example of how one kind of meat literally fits together. It's actually pretty simple: At the top of the animal, going from head to tail, are chuck, rib, short loin, sirloin, and round. At the underside of the animal, from front to back, are brisket, plate, and flank cuts. Shank cuts come from a cow's leg.

Different meats are naturally more fatty and tender than others and can be cooked more quickly. When an animal uses a muscle, it becomes leaner and, hence, tougher, such as cuts near the shoulder and the leg. Cuts in the middle, or belly of the cow, are more tender, such as the rib, loin, and plate. Tender cuts tend to be pricier at the grocery store. But even tough cuts of meat—such as brisket—can make for a wonderful meal. They just need to be cooked slowly, with moisture, at a low temperature. Note that ribs and steaks need to be cooked to at least medium rare, a minimum of 145°F. Read on to see how it all breaks down:

FROM THE FRONT AREA OF THE COW:

- **Chuck** is fatty, flavorful, and ideal for hamburgers.

- **Ribs** are juicy and tender, and work well on the barbecue. They can also be panfried.

- **Short loin** and **sirloin** cuts are often made into steaks to panfry, broil, or grill.

FROM A COW'S RUMP:

- **Round roasts** are low in fat and require long cooking times at low heat. Try these roasts in a slow cooker, roast them in an oven, or braise them.

- **Brisket** and **shank** cuts are both tough and need a low-heat, slow-cooking method.

- You can grill, braise, broil, or panfry **skirt** and **hanger** steaks, which come from the plate (also called the short plate).

- **Flank** steaks are very tough and need a moist-cooking method.

· HOW TO COOK A FEW OTHER · TYPES OF MEATS

Here are a few other simple preparations for common meats. Notice that we kept it simple and didn't get into the specifics of roasting lamb, smoking salmon, or making veal kabobs. We want you to get to that at some point, but first you need to know how to grill a hamburger.

WHAT TO DO WITH GROUND BEEF

Ground beef is great for hamburger patties on the grill and as a staple for simple meals like spaghetti, tacos, lasagna, and shepherd's pie. A little garlic salt does wonders for this type of meat, enhancing its natural flavor. To cook hamburgers, shape the ground beef into circular patties that are thin enough to cook all the way through, and barbecue on the grill. For other meals, you can brown the meat in a frying pan, stirring frequently as it goes from a bright-red color to brown. Cook ground meat to at least 160°F. When done, drain the grease and add it to the desired dish. The leaner the ground beef, the better it is for you (and also the more expensive). Watch grocery ads. You can almost always find ground beef on sale, especially the pricier and leaner grinds. When you find a really good sale, stock up and freeze (separating into meal-sized portions) whatever you have room for.

HOW TO PREPARE CHICKEN BREASTS

Boneless, skinless chicken breasts are widely available and a dream to cook with. (The butcher has done the work for you.) Because the chicken breasts have little fat, they can dry out, so you'll need to marinate them before grilling. Breasts are great baked in main dishes or shredded for casseroles and soups. Chicken wings, thighs, and drumsticks can all be cooked in a variety of yummy, flavorful ways, but nothing beats chicken breasts in terms of ease of preparation.

Elyssa adapted this easy way to cook chicken breasts in bulk in a slow cooker from a recipe by her friend Liz. She first sprinkles both sides with a hearty dose of Montreal Steak Seasoning (available in the seasoning aisle of most grocery stores) and layers as many fresh chicken breasts as she can fit in her slow cooker. She then adds about 1 cup of chicken stock, replaces the cover, and cooks them on low for 6 to 8 hours, or until they reach an internal temperature of 165°F. This flavorful chicken is great shredded in salads, enchiladas, soups, and just about anything else you care to throw it in. You can freeze the excess as whole breasts to thaw and shred later.

You can also grill, stir-fry, bake, and boil chicken. Just remember that it should turn completely white and must have an internal temperature of at least 165°F. And remember to be a fanatic about food safety (discussed later in this chapter).

❧ HOW TO COOK A ROAST

Elyssa's mother-in-law, MaryAnn, makes the perfect pot roast for Sunday dinners (of course she does!). The best part about it is that it's easy. Take a 2–3 pound rump or round roast and place in a slow cooker. Mix two packages of dehydrated onion soup with two cups of water and pour over roast. Cook a minimum of 8 hours on low heat, until the meat reaches an internal temperature of at least 160°F. After removing and carving the roast, you can use the drippings to make gravy. Simply add about ¼ cup diluted cornstarch (mix with a small amount of cold water so that the cornstarch liquefies) to about 2 to 3 cups of drippings. Season with salt and pepper to taste, and you've got a meal that would make any good pioneer woman proud.

❧ HOW TO COOK SALMON

Fish can be intimidating, even though it's low in fat and calories and loaded with nutrients. One thing that scares people away from fish is the bones. It's possible to purchase fish fillets without them, but it will cost you a bit more. You can also use tweezers to simply remove the tiny pin bones that may be left over in fillets. Make sure to purchase fish that smells fresh and is firm and free of discoloration. An easy way to start cooking fish is to purchase salmon fillets (about an inch thick) and barbecue them on the grill. Remove the skins, brush the fillets with olive oil, and sprinkle them with salt and pepper. Grill them on a grill preheated to medium to high heat. (Leave the cover open.) Fillets grill for 4–5 minutes and should be cooked to at least medium rare (145°F). They will be opaque when they are done.

HOW TO COOK A HAM

Ham comes from the hind leg of a pig, and is then aged, cured, smoked, or cooked. We like to buy fully cooked hams that come with a brown-sugar glaze, available at places such as Costco and Walmart. These are cooked in the oven for a set amount of time per pound (follow the directions on the packaging), and a brown-sugar glaze is applied near the end of cooking. Note that precooked ham needs to be reheated to 140°F.

HOW TO COOK A SWEET PORK ROAST

There are a number of ways to cook a pork roast. One of the easiest ways is to throw it in a slow cooker and roast it in a marinade (soy sauce and garlic, barbecue sauce). One of our favorite pork roast recipes is from the blog Favorite Family Recipes (www.favfamilyrecipes.com). It involves marinating pork in a cola and brown-sugar marinade, then cooking it in a slow cooker with chilies, enchilada sauce, and brown sugar. (See recipe at the end of this chapter.) Elyssa serves it atop a bed of lettuce, with black beans, cilantro rice (see recipe at the end of this chapter), sour cream, tomatoes, guacamole, and avocado-ranch salad dressing. It is delicious.

Note that meat will continue to cook after it is taken from its heat source, so remove from the heat when its 5–10°F lower than desired, says Chef Todd Leonard. (The bigger the cut, the more the temperature will rise. Be sure to test it with a thermometer.) Also, let all cooked meats rest before carving to give the juice time to redistribute. This will make your meats more moist and tender.

• WHEN TO USE TOFU •
(FOR VEGETARIANS AND MEAT EATERS)

Tofu is a vegetarian meat substitute made of soybean curd. Tofu itself has very little flavor or smell, making it ideal for both sweet and savory dishes. It will adapt to the recipe it's used in. Also, it's low in calories and fat but still filling. Elyssa loved tofu when she was a vegetarian and continues to love it today. She likes to use it when she makes Asian foods such as Pad Thai or miso soup. It's also delicious deep-fried in vegetable oil.

• ODE TO A SLOW COOKER •

It's certainly not the fanciest way to cook, but Elyssa and Natalie adore their slow cookers. The beauty of this kitchen gadget is that you can dump ingredients in it at the beginning of the day, cook them over high heat from three to seven hours or low heat from five to eight hours (or more), and at dinnertime have a delicious meal waiting for you. This is particularly useful on hectic days when you know you won't have time to cook dinner, and it's nice for Sundays because you can eat immediately after church without a lot of preparation time. Also, it's hard to mess things up in a slow cooker. (Unless you forget to plug it in or turn it on, which both Natalie and Elyssa have done on a handful of occasions.) If you don't have a slow cooker, we strongly advise you to acquire one soon. It's helpful to purchase one that has a built-in timer so that you can cook things for an exact amount of time even when you have to be away from your home all day long. See the end of this chapter for ridiculously easy slow-cooker recipes.

• PRESENTATION •

Before you eat with your stomach, you eat with your eyes, and it's worth the extra time to make food look appetizing to those who will consume it. Keep fresh parsley and herbs on hand for garnish and invest in some pretty serving dishes and platters. Think of yourself as an artist and the plate as your palette, using the bright colors available in nature's bounty to create something beautiful. (An added benefit of choosing brightly colored foods is that they are typically nutrient-rich, from bright green spinach leaves to beautifully orange sweet potatoes to bright red strawberries.) Even a simple scattering of Parmesan cheese can dress up an otherwise ordinary-looking plate of spaghetti. Natalie finds it much easier to keep portions under control when she dishes up entrées and garnishes them rather than serving food buffet-style.

Have the temperature of your plates match the temperature of your food, says Chef Todd Leonard. Warm up plates for hot dishes, and chill plates for cool ones.

• BE SAFE! •

One of the most important things you need to know about cooking is how to protect yourself from food-borne illnesses. It only takes one really bad case of food poisoning to make someone a believer in hand-washing and safe food-handling practices. On Elyssa's twenty-eighth birthday, she got bad food poisoning—probably from a takeout Mexican salad—and ended up in the emergency room. She lived to tell about it, but to this day, she can't eat Mexican food and birthday cake on the same day.

One out of every four people each year will have a food-borne illness, says Shelley Feist,[2] executive director of the national nonprofit Partnership for Food Safety Education (PFSE). Based in Washington, DC, her organization works to educate the public on safe food-handling practices. Basically, they want to save us from ourselves and from sloppy kitchen habits that can make everyone sick.

"The consumer is the last line of the food chain," says Feist. "It's very important that they do what they can to reduce their risk once they take home food from the restaurant or the retail market." Young children, the elderly, pregnant women, and those with compromised immune systems are particularly at risk for food-borne illness. But anyone who cooks should use the following four core practices recommended by the PFSE: clean, separate, cook, and chill.

Here's a look at each of these practices as recommended on the PFSE website, www.fightbac.org.[3] The information is used with their permission.

CLEAN

Wash your hands, already! Although you can't see or smell bacteria, it can be lurking all over hands, kitchen surfaces, countertops, cutting boards, and sinks. To fight back, (or fight bac, as the PFSE campaign suggests):

- Wash your hands with warm water and soap for *at least* twenty seconds before and after handling food.

- Keep the kitchen surfaces clean. Wash surfaces, cutting boards, and dishes after use with warm, soapy water. From time to time, you can also sanitize your cutting boards and surfaces by using a couple drops of unscented bleach mixed with water.

- Rinse fruits and vegetables, even those with skins that are not eaten. Firm-skinned fruits and vegetables should be scrubbed clean with a brush under running water.

SEPARATE

Bacteria can be easily spread from one food item to another, and from one surface to another. This is why it's absolutely essential that you start

63

with a clean, sanitized cooking area. Also, you need to keep raw meats and their juices away from prepared foods. You don't want the juice from a raw turkey, for example, getting near your Thanksgiving Day potatoes. Also remember:

- Separation starts at the grocery store. Keep the raw meat, poultry, seafood and eggs in your cart away from other foods, and in the grocery bags. Once you've come home, keep these foods away from other foods in the refrigerator.

- Don't cut meat and vegetables on the same cutting board without first cleaning and sanitizing it. It's helpful to purchase two cutting boards and to always have one designated for meats, and another for vegetables and other items.

- Any plate or surface that has held raw beef, poultry, fish, or eggs needs to be promptly washed and sanitized. Never reuse a dirty plate for cooked food.

∽ COOK

Heating raw foods to the proper temperature will kill the bacteria that can make you sick. One of the biggest mistakes consumers make, says Shelley Feist of the nonprofit Partnership for Food Safety Education, is guessing the temperature of a food instead of actually using a food thermometer. These small devices can be purchased at grocery stores and culinary specialty stores and are inexpensive and easy to use. Not only do they keep your food safe, they may also make it taste better too. Feist says people who "guess" at doneness often overcook food, making it tough, chewy, or burnt when it could be moist and tender. Here are some other things to consider:

- Cook roasts and steaks to a minimum of 145°F. Cook poultry to the safe minimum internal temperature of 165°F (check the innermost thigh and wing, or the thickest part of the breast). Cook ground meat to at least 160°F. Cook fish to 145°F or until the flesh is opaque and the meat shreds easily.

- Eggs need to be cooked until the yolks are firm, not runny. Do not use recipes that include raw eggs in the finished product.

- Microwave cooking can be uneven and leave cold spots where bacteria can remain. Make sure to check for these, and to rotate food cooked in a microwave.

- Even leftovers need to be properly reheated, to at least 165°F. Gravies, sauces, and soups should be brought to a boil again.

CHILL

Quickly cooling foods will stop the growth of the bacteria that can make you sick. To do so, as soon as you get home from the store, place items in a refrigerator that maintains a temperature of 40°F or below. Don't know how cold your refrigerator is? You can buy a small appliance thermometer at a hardware store and easily check. Your freezer should be at 0°F or below, says the PFSE. Also keep in mind:

- Two hours is the maximum amount of time that raw meat, poultry, and eggs can sit out at room temperature without being refrigerated or frozen. After that, you'll have to throw them away. Same goes for cooked food and fresh fruits and vegetables that have been cut into. If the temperature is above 90°F—if you are outside, for example—food can only sit out for an hour.

- There are three acceptable ways to defrost food, and setting it on the counter to thaw at room temperature is NOT one of them. To be safe, defrost in the fridge, the microwave, or in cold water.

MARINATE FOODS IN THE REFRIGERATOR

- Store foods in small containers in the fridge so that they will cool faster. This may mean that you need to transfer them from the containers they were originally cooked or served in.

- Enjoy the peace of mind that comes from regularly cleaning out the fridge and getting rid of old food.

THE PARTNERSHIP FOR FOOD SAFETY EDUCATION'S
SAFE COOKING CHART[4]

*Safe Cooking Temperatures—as measured with a food thermometer

GROUND MEAT & MEAT MIXTURES	
Beef, Pork, Veal, Lamb	160°F
Turkey, Chicken	165°F
FRESH BEEF, VEAL, LAMB	
Medium Rare	145°F
Medium	160°F
Well Done	170°F
POULTRY	
Chicken & Turkey (whole)	165°F
Poultry Parts	165°F
Duck & Goose	165°F
Stuffing (cooked alone or in bird)	165°F
FRESH PORK	
Medium	160°F
Well Done	170°F
HAM	
Fresh (raw)	160°F
Precooked (to reheat)	140°F
EGGS & EGG DISHES	
Eggs	cook until yolk & whites are firm
Egg Dishes	160°F
SEAFOOD	
Fin Fish	145°F or until opaque & flakes easily
Shrimp, Lobster & Crabs	Flesh pearly & opaque
Clams, Oysters & Mussels	Shells open during cooking
Scallops	Milky white or opaque & firm
LEFTOVERS	
Leftovers & Casseroles	165°F

• WHAT IN THE WORLD? •

Ever read a recipe and have no idea what a certain ingredient is? This has happened to us on many occasions, and fortunately the Internet makes it possible to research even the most obscure components of a recipe. (If you don't recognize many of the ingredients in a recipe, it may be a good sign that you need to try something simpler.) Or maybe it's the dish in general that is mystifying. Either way, here are just a handful of foods you may want to know about. At the very least, you can throw around the terms *arugula* and *gremolata* to impress your friends.

- ✍ **ANCHOVY:** A very fishy, strong-smelling, and stong-tasting saltwater fish. Anchovies are small and are usually packaged in cans of oil.

- ✍ **ARUGULA:** A gritty salad green commonly used in many Italian salads. It has a strong flavor and is often sold in specialty markets and sometimes in grocery stores. It's also sometimes called rocket, rocket salad, or roquette.

- ✍ **BALSAMIC VINEGAR:** A dark, sweet vinegar that has been aged. It's made from a white grape. Other types of vinegar include cider, red wine, rice, and white wine.

- ✍ **BASMATI RICE:** A long-grain rice with a nutty flavor favored in Indian cuisines. Other types of rice include Arborio (a medium-grain Italian rice), brown rice (nutty and chewy), instant (partially cooked then dehydrated), and risotto (see separate entry below).

- ✍ **BÉARNAISE SAUCE:** A zingy sauce that includes butter, egg yolk, vinegar, and tarragon. It is similar to a hollandaise sauce.

- ✍ **BEURRE BLANC:** "White butter" in French. A creamy sauce is made by combining a wine, vinegar, and shallot reduction with cold butter.

- ✍ **BETTY:** A baked fruit dessert topped with buttered bread crumbs.

- ✍ **BORSCHT:** A beet soup that originated in Poland and Russia.

෨෪ **BOUILLON:** Clear broth made by simmering chicken, beef, veal, shrimp, or vegetables. You can buy bouillon cubes at grocery stores as well.

෨෪ **BREAD FLOUR**: Flour made from hard wheat. It is better for bread making than all-purpose flour. You can typically find it at the grocery store or purchase it from a flour mill.

෨෪ **BUTTERMILK:** Milk made by culturing skim or part-skim milk with bacteria. It adds zip to baked goods.

෨෪ **CAPERS:** A small, round food from the flower bud of a Caper bush in the Mediterranean. They are used as a garnish and in sauces and are generally brined or salted.

෨෪ **CHILI:** The pod part of a pepper plant. Types range from the mild Anaheim chili to the hotter chipotle and serrano peppers. Some other types of chilies are ancho (mild to medium hot), green (mild), pepperoncini (medium to medium hot), and poblano (mild to medium hot).

෨෪ **CHIVES:** Mild herbs that have an onion or garlic flavor. These herbs have long green leaves.

෨෪ **CHORIZO:** A spicy pork sausage used in both Mexican and Spanish cuisine.

෨෪ **CHUTNEY:** Relish made from fruits or vegetables. These relishes can be sweet or hot, or both.

෨෪ **CONSOMMÉ:** A clarified stock made using the liquid derived from simmering meat, fish, or poultry, and their bones.

෨෪ **CORNSTARCH:** A thickening agent that can be used in place of flour (sauces will be opaque, not white). It comes from a part of the corn kernel.

෨෪ **COUSCOUS:** Granular semolina (coarsely ground wheat). It's a favorite in African dishes.

CRÈME FRAÎCHE: A thick dairy product made from heavy cream soured with a bacterial culture.

DIJON MUSTARD: A tangy, intense mustard made from brown or black mustard seeds and white wine.

EVAPORATED MILK: Canned milk made from fresh milk, but with 60 percent of the water removed. You can purchase whole, low-fat, and skim versions of evaporated milk. Because the milk has been heat sterilized, it does not need to be refrigerated until it is opened.

GIBLETS: (Do you really want to know this?) The insides of poultry, including the gizzard, heart, and liver. Often used to make gravy.

GNOCCHI: Italian dumplings typically made from flour, puff pastry, or potatoes. The dough is most often shaped into small balls and then boiled in water. It's frequently served with a cream or butter sauce, Parmesan cheese, and sometimes spinach.

GREMOLATA: A combination of garlic, lemon peel, and chopped parsley added to dishes to intensify their flavor.

HEAVY CREAM: A dense, rich cream that has 36–40 percent butterfat. It's often used to make whipped cream and will double in volume when whipped. It's also sometimes referred to as heavy whipping cream when sold commercially.

HOLLANDAISE SAUCE: A rich, buttery sauce made with, you guessed it, butter, egg yolk, and lemon juice. It's popular served with fish, eggs, and vegetables.

HUMMUS: A spread made from ground, cooked garbanzo beans. It is often seasoned with lemon juice and oil.

JICAMA: Similar in appearance to a potato, jicama is a root vegetable with a brown skin, crisp, crunchy white insides, and a sweet taste. It is used in many Mexican dishes.

KEY LIME: A small, tart lime with a yellow-green skin. This lime is grown in Florida and is a main ingredient in key lime pie.

KOSHER SALT: A coarse-grain salt used for preparing food. It's an excellent cooking salt because of its texture, and it is free of additives.

LARD: Popular in some Mexican cuisines, lard is a saturated fat made from refined pork fat.

MIREPOIX: A French term for chopped onions, carrots, and celery. It can either be used raw or sautéed in butter, and is often used to flavor stocks and stews or other dishes.

MUSHROOMS: Surely you know these fungi and would recognize button mushrooms commonly sold at the grocery store. But did you know that other kinds include cremini, enoki, oyster, porcini, portobello, and shiitake?

PÂTÉ: An appetizer made of ground meat and fat that is formed into a spreadable paste.

PESTO: A green-colored sauce made from basil, olive oil, garlic, Parmesan cheese, and pine nuts (optional). It's used in many Italian dishes.

PECTIN: Found naturally in some fruits and vegetables, this substance is used to thicken jams, jellies, and preserves. You can buy commercial pectin at the grocery store or at a store that sells canning supplies.

PHYLLO: Also called "filo," this Greek pastry dough is thin, super flaky, and most often cut into sheets. It's made from water and flour and can be purchased commercially.

PILAF: A rice dish in which rice is browned in fat and then cooked with broth and seasonings.

PINE NUTS: Tiny nuts that are white in color and that come from certain varieties of pine trees. This is a favorite in Mediterranean dishes.

🐦 **POLENTA:** A cake or mush made from cornmeal and served in many Italian dishes. You can fry polenta, and it's very tasty with Parmesan cheese.

🐦 **PROSCIUTTO:** The Italian word for "ham." Outside Italy, it typically refers to cured ham sliced very thin and eaten uncooked. Sometimes it is lightly cooked, especially when served in pastas.

🐦 **QUINOA:** This grainlike crop is native to the Andes Mountains of Bolivia, Chile, and Peru and is very nutritious. In the United States, it is often sold in whole-grain formula so it can be cooked like rice.

🐦 **RISOTTO:** An Italian rice dish in which rice is blended with stock and stirred continually. It is often flavored with Parmesan cheese.

🐦 **SCALLIONS:** Sometimes referred to as green onions, scallions have long, thin green stems and small white bottoms.

🐦 **SHALLOT:** A member of the onion family shaped something like garlic, with multiple cloves.

🐦 **SWEETENED CONDENSED MILK:** A combination of whole milk and sugar that is then evaporated to make the resulting product very dense and sweet. It's often used in candies and bakery items.

🐦 **SUN-DRIED TOMATOES:** Small, sun-withered tomatoes that lend a strong flavor to recipes. They are sold packed in oil or packaged in plastic.

🐦 **TOMATILLOS:** Also called "tomato verde" (green tomato) in Spanish, the tomatillo is a member of the nightshade family and is related to the tomato. These plants are green, range in size from a large cherry tomato to the size of a large lime, and grow to maturity in husks. They are a staple in Mexican cuisine and are used to make salsa verde (green salsa).

🐦 **TRUFFLE:** Truffles refer to a rich, creamy candy made of chocolate, as well as to a fungus that you can eat. If you see the word *truffle* in a savory dish on a menu, it probably refers to the edible fungus.

• WHAT'S IT ALL MEAN? •

Cookbooks, recipes, food blogs, and cooking shows often throw around culinary terms as if everyone knows the difference between al forno and al dente. Thanks to the Internet, it's possible to find the definition of pretty much any dish, ingredient, or cooking method you come across. (No need to tearfully call your mom.) Cooking is certainly not a place to guess at a definition—you'll be in a world of hurt if you confuse scald, which involves cooking, with score, which involves cutting. In addition to the cooking and cutting terms listed earlier in this chapter, here are some common culinary terms you need know:

- **AL DENTE** (adj.): In Italian this phrase means "to the tooth." It's a term—generally used for pasta—for food that retains a slight firmness when bitten. Foods that are al dente are not mushy or soft.

- **AL FORNO** (adj.): An Italian phrase for "roasted" or "baked."

- **AU GRATIN** (adj.): A food that has a crisp crust (usually cooked under a broiler), often topped with cheese or bread crumbs.

- **AU JUS** (adj.): A French phrase signifying meat served with its own juices.

- **BASTE** (v.): To spoon liquid (such as juices) over food during the cooking process in order to retain moisture.

- **BLANCH** (v.): To quickly submerge food into boiling water, followed by cold water, to stop the cooking process. This is done in order to preserve color and texture, and to loosen skins.

- **BONE-IN** (adj.): Refers to cuts of meat or poultry that still have a bone.

- **BROWN** (v.): To literally cause the surface of meat to turn brown by cooking rapidly over high heat.

- **BUTTERFLY** (v.): To slice something nearly in half to form a butterfly shape.

- **CARAMELIZE** (v.): To melt sugar until it liquefies to become a brown, caramel-flavored syrup. Alternately, you can place sugar on top of a food and place it directly under a heat source until it caramelizes.

- **COAT** (v.): To cover something with a thin layer.

CRUMBLE (v.): To break food up into pieces. As a noun, *crumble* refers to a dessert with a crumbly topping made of sugar and flour.

CUT IN (v.): To add fat (such as butter) to a dry ingredient. This is usually done with a fork or pastry blender. You can even do it with your fingers.

DASH (n.): A very small amount of an ingredient thrown into a dish, generally less than ⅛ of a teaspoon.

DEGLAZE (v.): To add a small amount of liquid to a skillet following cooking in order to loosen the cooked bits of food stuck to the pan. This is an excellent way to make a base for a stock, sauce, or gravy.

DRIZZLE (v.): To pour a liquid (such as melted chocolate) in a thin line over food.

FOLD (v.): To gently combine ingredients, often using a spatula. In this process, no air is removed.

GARNISH (v.): To decorate using food.

HULL (v.): To use a knife to take off stems and leaves.

HUSK (v.): To remove the outer shell or leaves of an item, such as corn on the cob.

KNEAD (v.): To make dough smooth and elastic by pressing or punching it with one's hands, or using an electric dough mixer.

MARINATE (v.): To augment a food's natural flavors and tenderness by soaking in a liquid mixture, called a marinade, usually for several hours. This is often done with meats.

PUREE (v.): To liquefy a solid using a blender or food processor.

REDUCE (v.): To literally reduce the amount of a liquid through evaporation in order to enhance the flavor. This is done by boiling the liquid, uncovered, on the stove.

ROLLING BOIL (n.): A type of boil so rapid that you can't stir it away.

RUB (n.): A mixture of spices and seasonings rubbed on meat or poultry (and even vegetables) before cooking.

SCALD (v.): To heat a liquid to just below its boiling point. This word is also sometimes interchanged with blanch, which means to plunge rapidly in boiling water.

SCORE (v.): To make shallow cuts on the surface of a food, using a knife. This can be done to enhance flavor, appearance, or both.

73

SHELL (v.): To remove something's shell. For instance, you could shell a lobster, shell peas, or shell walnuts.

SHRED (v.): To cut food into thin strips. This can be done by hand or with a grater. You can also use a food processor to shred food.

SKIM (v.): To take off undesirable residue from the top of a liquid.

STRAIN (v.): To remove undesirable particles (and sometimes water) from food by running it through a strainer or sieve.

TOSS (v.): To gently mix together items, such as the ingredients used in a salad.

ZEST (n.): The outermost layer of citrus fruits. As a verb, zest means to remove this layer using a knife or citrus zester.

• RECIPES •

Included in this section are some of Elyssa and Natalie's favorite recipes. Most of these are basic recipes with few steps, making them ideal for beginners. Don't, however, let the simplicity of these recipes fool you. They may be easy to make, but they are hard to pass up. Enjoy!

DIVINE ROASTED VEGETABLES

2 Tbsp. olive oil

2 lbs. root vegetables, washed and cut
(carrots, potatoes, red onions, squash)

2 Tbsp. garlic, minced

½ Tbsp. seasoning salt

1 tsp. thyme

1 tsp. basil

Combine ingredients in a large bowl, mixing to coat thoroughly. Roast at 450°F for 20 to 25 minutes, increasing time to 35 minutes if potatoes are used. Turn vegetables halfway through the cooking process.

CHERRY FRUIT DIP

1 (8-oz.) package cream cheese

1 (7-oz.) jar marshmallow cream

2 tsp. maraschino cherry juice

Soften cream cheese and combine with marshmallow cream until smooth. Add maraschino juice. Refrigerate until serving.

CORN SALSA

½ bunch cilantro

2 large tomatoes

3 avocados

1 (15-oz.) can corn, drained

1 (15-oz.) can black beans, rinsed and drained

2 tablespoons lime juice

1 pkg. dry Italian dressing mix

¼ cup vinegar

3 Tbsp. water

½ cup vegetable oil

Wash cilantro and chop into small pieces. Wash tomatoes and chop into small pieces about 1-inch thick. Chop avocados to same size. Combine corn, black beans, cilantro, avocado, lime juice, and tomatoes. Prepare Italian dressing mix according to directions on box, using vinegar, water, and oil. Fold into other ingredients. Refrigerate before serving.

— *Adapted from a recipe by Michelle Watabe, of Highlands Ranch, Colorado*

CILANTRO-LIME RICE

1 cup uncooked rice (long-grain, white rice)

1 tsp. butter or margarine

2 cloves garlic, minced

1 tsp. lime juice

1 (15-oz.) can chicken broth

1 cup water

1 Tbsp. lime juice

2 tsp. sugar

3 Tbsp. fresh chopped cilantro

In a saucepan, combine rice, butter, garlic, 1 teaspoon lime juice, chicken broth, and water. Bring to a boil. Cover and cook on low 15–20 minutes, until rice is tender. Remove from heat. In a small bowl, combine remaining lime juice, sugar, and cilantro. Pour over hot cooked rice and mix in as you fluff the rice.

—*Courtesy Favorite Family Recipes blog, www.favfamilyrecipes.com*

SOUTHWESTERN SALAD

2 heads romaine lettuce,
   washed and torn into bite-size pieces

2 cups boneless, skinless chicken breast,
   cooked and shredded (optional)

1 (14-oz.) can black beans, rinsed and drained

1 tomato, diced

1 (14-oz) can corn, drained

1 small can sliced olives,
   rinsed and drained

1 bunch green onions, sliced

1 bottle ranch dressing

barbecue sauce, for drizzling

Toss together salad ingredients in a large bowl. Drizzle with barbecue sauce and ranch dressing. Serve with tortilla chips or cornbread.

SLOW-COOKED RIBS

3-4 lbs. country-style pork ribs

2 cups barbecue sauce

1 onion, diced

sliced red and green peppers (optional

2 tsp. lemon juice

pineapple chunks (optional)

Place ribs in a slow cooker. Combine remaining ingredients in separate bowl. Pour over ribs. Cook on low for 8–10 hours.

SLOW COOKER CHICKEN BREASTS

6 boneless, skinless chicken breasts

1 cup chicken stock

Montreal Steak Seasoning, to taste

Trim fat from chicken breasts. One by one, coat each side with a hearty dose of Montreal Steak Seasoning. Layer in slow cooker. Add chicken stock. Cook on low for 5–8 hours, until chicken reaches an internal temperature of 165°F. Shred if you plan to use immediately. Keep as whole breasts if you intend to freeze.

—Adapted from a recipe by Liz Christensen of Cedar Hills, Utah

ELYSSA'S GUACAMOLE

4 ripe avocados

sea salt to taste

juice of ½ lime

cayenne pepper to taste

Mash avocados with a fork. Add juice of ½ lime. Season with sea salt and cayenne pepper to taste. (Add the pepper slowly so that you don't make it unbearably spicy.)

SWEET PORK ROAST

2 lbs. pork (we use boneless pork rib meat)

3 cans cola (NOT diet)

¼ cup brown sugar

dash garlic salt

¼ cup water

1 can diced green chiles

1 cup brown sugar

¾ can red enchilada sauce, medium

Put the pork in a heavy-duty ziplock plastic bag to marinate. Add about a can and a half of cola and about ¼ cup of brown sugar. Marinate for a few hours or overnight.

Drain marinade and put pork, ½ can of cola, water, and garlic salt in slow cooker on high for 3–4 hours (or until it shreds easily, but don't let it get TOO dry) or on low for 8 hours. Remove pork from slow cooker and drain any liquid left in the pot. Shred pork.

In a food processor or blender, blend ½ can cola, chiles, enchilada sauce, and remaining brown sugar (about a cup; you can add a little more or less to taste). If it looks too thick, add more cola little by little. Put shredded pork and sauce in slow cooker and cook on low for 2 hours. Serve with shredded lettuce, black beans, rice, sour cream, and guacamole for a delicious salad.

—Courtesy Favorite Family Recipes blog, www.favfamilyrecipes.com

PHILLY FRENCH DIP SANDWICHES

2-lb. rump roast

3 (10.5-oz.) cans consommé

6 hoagie rolls

12 slices provolone cheese

yellow bell pepper

red bell pepper

2 cups chopped mushrooms

2 Tbsp. butter

salt and pepper to taste

Pour consommé over top of roast and cook in slow cooker on low for 8–10 hours. When finished cooking, let roast rest and then shred. Meanwhile, chop peppers and sauté with mushrooms in butter. Sprinkle with salt and pepper. Split hoagie rolls in half and line each half with provolone cheese. Broil in the oven until cheese is bubbly and bread is lightly browned (watch closely to prevent burning). To assemble sandwiches, line bottom half with mushrooms, peppers and shredded beef. Top with top bun. Pour consommé through a sieve to strain, then distribute into individual ramekins to make an au jus sauce.

FUNERAL POTATOES

1 (32-oz.) bag frozen hash browns
  (we like cubed "homestyle")

2 (10.5-oz.) cans cream of chicken soup

1 soup can of milk

1 (8-oz.) container sour cream

1½ cups shredded cheddar

1 tsp. salt

2 cups cornflakes, crushed

⅓ cup melted butter

Preheat oven to 350°F. Combine all ingredients except margarine and cornflakes and put in a 9-inch by 13-inch baking dish that has been sprayed with cooking spray. Combine cornflakes and melted butter and pour over top. Bake at 350°F for one hour.

WHITE BEAN CHICKEN CHILI

Serves 12–16 people (depending on serving size)

2 Tbsp. butter

3 tsp. garlic powder

2 medium or 1 large yellow onion

2 lbs. boneless, skinless chicken breasts, cut into pieces

5 (15-oz.) cans great northern beans

1 (36-oz.) carton chicken stock

2 (4-oz.) cans chopped green chilies

2 tsp. cumin

2 tsp. oregano

2 tsp sea salt

½ tsp. pepper

½ tsp. cayenne pepper
 (more if desired)

1 cup heavy whipping cream

2 cups sour cream

¾ cup salsa verde (green salsa)

Chop onion and chicken and sauté in butter and garlic salt in a large pot, over medium heat. Drain and rinse white beans, then add beans, chicken stock, chilies, cumin, oregano, and sea salt to pot. Simmer for 30 minutes, or for a couple of hours, depending on when you need it.

Remove from heat and add pepper, cayenne pepper, sour cream, heavy cream, and salsa verde.

—*Adapted from a recipe by Staci Sadler, of Cedar Hills, Utah*

BAKED ZITI

1 (16-oz.) pkg. ziti or penne pasta

2 yellow onions, chopped

1 lb. lean ground beef or Italian sausage

2 (16-oz.) bottles spaghetti sauce

2 tbsp. Italian seasoning (optional)

6 oz. provolone cheese, sliced

1½ cups sour cream

6 oz. mozzarella cheese, shredded

2 Tbsp. grated parmesan cheese

Boil pasta until al dente. Drain well. Lightly butter a 9-inch by 13-inch (or larger) baking dish. Over medium heat in a large saucepan, cook onions until transparent. Add ground beef and brown until pink is gone. Add spaghetti sauce and stir in seasoning. Warm until bubbly. Layer half of the pasta in a baking dish. Add sliced provolone for the second layer and sour cream for the third layer. The fourth layer is half of the sauce. Repeat layers with pasta, mozzarella and remaining sauce. Top with grated Parmesan. Bake at 350°F for 30 minutes, or until warm and bubbly. Serve with garlic bread.

SWEET SALMON

whole salmon, cut into large portions

juice of one fresh lemon

2 tsp. dry mustard

⅔ cup brown sugar

Cover a large baking sheet with aluminum foil. Place salmon on top and sprinkle with lemon juice and mustard. Pat with brown sugar to ¼-inch thickness. Fold foil over, creating a sealed packet. Barbecue or bake in a 400-degree oven 15 to 20 minutes, or until flesh flakes easily.

CHICKEN CURRY IN A HURRY

2 Tbsp. flour

1 tsp. salt

½ tsp. cayenne pepper
(or less if you'd like)

1 lb. boneless, skinless chicken breasts,
cut into 1½-inch pieces

1 Tbsp. curry powder

2 Tbsp. canola oil

1 medium onion, thinly sliced

2 garlic cloves, minced

1 cup chicken broth

1½ Tbsp. tomato paste

¼ cup cilantro, chopped

⅓ cup plain non-fat yogurt

Mix flour, salt, and cayenne pepper in a ziplock plastic bag. Using a paper towel, pat excess moisture off chicken. Add chicken to bag in small batches, shaking to coat each batch. Heat oil in a large skillet over medium heat. Add chicken and cook until lightly browned. Add curry powder and toss to coat. Remove chicken from heat. Add onion and garlic to pan and cook 2 minutes. Add broth and tomato paste, stirring well to incorporate. Return chicken to pan and simmer uncovered about 8 minutes, or until chicken is cooked through and sauce reduced. Stir in yogurt. Garnish with cilantro when serving.

—*Adapted from a recipe on allrecipes.com*

BEACH STREET CHICKEN LINGUINE

Marinade:

½ cup olive oil

2 cloves garlic, crushed

2 tablespoons Cajun seasoning

juice of one lemon (or ¼ cup bottled lemon juice)

2 tablespoons minced fresh parsley

¼ cup brown sugar

3 Tbsp. soy sauce

2 chicken breasts, sliced

Pasta:

1 (16-oz.) pkg. linguine

2 Tbsp. olive oil

zest from one lemon

juice from one lemon

¼ cup chopped fresh parsley

salt and freshly ground pepper

½ cup grated parmesan cheese

3 green onions, chopped
(white and green parts)

Combine the marinade ingredients in a bowl and whisk lightly before pouring into a ziplock plastic bag. Pat chicken dry and toss in marinade to coat. Refrigerate 3-12 hours.

When ready to cook, preheat skillet over medium heat and pour marinade and chicken into the skillet. Saute over medium-high heat until chicken is cooked and marinade comes to a boil.

Combine juice of one lemon, lemon zest, olive oil, green onions, and fresh parsley together in a small bowl. Set aside.

While the chicken is sauteing, cook linguine in boiling water until done. Drain and return to warm pot. Pour lemon juice/olive oil/green onion mixture over pasta and mix lightly. When chicken is finished cooking, add hot pasta mixture to the skillet with the chicken and toss well. Sprinkle with salt and pepper to taste and toss in Parmesan cheese. Garnish with additional lemon zest and fresh parsley. Serve warm.

—Courtesy Deals to Meals blog, dealstomeals.blogspot.com

· BAKING BLISS ·

Not many things can deflate a mood more quickly than a loaf of bread that fails to properly rise. Brownies that stubbornly stay raw in the middle or chocolate chip cookies that spread as big as Texas likely qualify as runners-up.

Baking failures are often monumental and memorable. Take Elyssa's holiday bread pudding fiasco, for example. Or the time Natalie made carrot cake cupcakes for a bridal shower only to have them implode fifteen minutes before the party was scheduled to start. Few things are as frustrating as spending precious time tied up in apron strings only to have the finished product go kaput.

· IF AT FIRST YOU DON'T SUCCEED, · TRY, TRY AGAIN

True, taking raw ingredients, such as flour, sugar, butter, and eggs, and combining them into a delectable finished product takes time and practice. But learning how to bake isn't a half-baked idea. Crafting your own breads, cakes, and cookies can save major dough in your grocery budget, especially if you bake with items from your usable food storage (the LDS Church has long counseled membership to store versatile grains like wheat; see chapter six for more details). Fresh-from-the-oven goodies will delight your friends and family, whose rave reviews of your products will help your kitchen confidence rise like the tops of your perfectly formed whole wheat bread loaves.

All you need to get started is a short lesson in baking basics. Next thing you know, it will all be a piece of cake.

• SCRATCH THAT •

There are many reasons people list for shunning from-scratch baking. You've likely uttered a few of these excuses yourself (we know we have!). "I don't have time to bake." "I don't follow recipes well." "I get unpredictable results." And a favorite—"It is too expensive to make things from scratch."

Each of these defenses has a legitimate argument behind it. But we bet you a batch of homemade chocolate sandwich cookies with thick cream-cheese filling that you can bake nearly everything your heart desires, easily, at home, with only a small investment of time and money.

Don't believe us? Consider this. Already-prepared brownies bought from a store bakery are typically triple or quadruple the cost of a one-dollar mix of the just-add-egg-and-oil variety. But using the cocoa, flour, sugar, eggs, and vanilla already residing in your kitchen pantry is cheaper still. Whisking together the ingredients by hand or throwing them into a mixer adds only minutes to the entire process. (Even less if you follow our timesaving tips at the end of this chapter to create your own premade mixes). And you didn't have to make a trip to the grocery store.

"Usually when you have to make a quick trip to the grocery store, you end up buying all these things that you really didn't have to get," says Mindy Spencer, co-owner of Pantry Secrets, a Utah company that produces instructional cooking and baking DVDs and products. "When you make things at home, you're saving the time that you would've spent to get to the store, the gas money to get there, plus the extra money that you would've spent while you were there."[1]

• PROOF IS IN THE PUDDING •

A cost-savings comparison is stark when it comes to more pricey baked goods, such as 100-percent whole wheat bread. What can cost several dollars per loaf at grocery store or bakery can be made at home for pennies, especially if you grind your own wheat, says Jeannie Tuckett Dayton,[2] who runs Pantry Secrets with her daughter Mindy.

The one-time cost of the ingredients may run higher than buying a premade package. But once you have the basic ingredients and tools on hand, you are good to go for many batches.

• IT'S TOOL TIME •

If you're going to spend any amount of time baking, you'll want a handful of essential implements on hand. (Okay, there are more than a handful.) Start with what you will use the most and add to your collection of baking tools over the years, as you can afford them. We've noted what devices can pull double duty to minimize your out-of-pocket cost. (This list is also found in chapter two, sans notes).

↩ MEASURING

- ❧ steel or plastic measuring cups
- ❧ 2-cup glass measuring cup (like Pyrex brand, for measuring wet ingredients)

- 8-cup glass measuring bowl
- measuring spoons (inexpensive; two sets are nice to have)

CONTAINERS AND PANS

- stainless-steel mixing bowls
- plastic bowls
- ½-sheet pans (several)
- rectangular cake pan
- 2 cupcake pans
- 2 round cake pans (for double-layer cakes)
- Bundt cake pan (or angel food cake pan)
- springform pan (or specialty cheesecake pan)
- loaf pans for bread (pick a size that you like best)
- casserole dishes (9 x 13 glass pans)
- cooling racks (We like the rectangular kind with small openings so goodies don't fall through.

SPOONS AND TOOLS

- wooden spoons
- whisks (heavy-duty and "balloon")
- spatulas (including one for removing cookies from a baking sheet)
- candy thermometer
- grater
- microplane (for zesting lemons or grating nutmeg)
- cookie cutters
- ice cream scoop or cookie scoop (for making uniform cookies)

- ✤ rolling pin
- ✤ pastry blender

· A WORD ON APPLIANCES ·

In order to truly apply yourself in the kitchen, it may be handy to have a small appliance or two on hand. If you don't have room in your budget or kitchen for these things, don't sweat it. Actually, do sweat it—all of these machines have a do-it-by-hand component that will also get the job done.

> **JUICER:** You can buy an automatic juicer for as cheap as ten dollars, or a hand juicer for a few bucks less.

> **HAND MIXER:** The motors on these burn out quick, so don't invest a lot of money. Purchase one made by a reliable brand and with a few speed settings. Use a whisk or spoon to incorporate ingredients if you don't have one.

> **FOOD PROCESSOR:** These are great for making flaky pastries, chopping nuts, and a multitude of other sweet and savory applications. You can use a pastry blender or knife instead, but it will take longer.

> **ELECTRIC KETTLE:** This is handy for more than hot chocolate. A quick-heating kettle can boil water in less than a minute, which is great for recipes that call for really hot water.

· STAND-UP KIND OF GAL ·

Probably the most expensive small appliance you'll buy for your kitchen will be a stand mixer. There are many brands available; two well-known makers are KitchenAid or Bosch. Breville, Blendtec, Hamilton Beach, and a host of other manufacturers also make good-quality mixers.

Shop around before you make a purchase. Read reviews online and ask friends and neighbors for their opinions. Elyssa has a KitchenAid and loves it. Natalie adores her Bosch. Think about what you'll really use a stand mixer for. Will you be kneading bread? Making cookies? Mixing cake batter? Whipping egg whites? Be sure the machine you purchase can do what you'll need it to, or will do so with added accessories.

· SET UP FOR SUCCESS ·

YOUR BAKING CENTER

The time required to bake at home is often greatly exaggerated by those who have experienced one too many failures in the kitchen. Baking from scratch really isn't that time-consuming, unless you're making a particularly high-maintenance product, like chocolate soufflé.

There are ways to reduce your time investment significantly. For instance, organization and baking experts alike agree that efficient kitchen organization is a must if you're going to bake frequently. Whenever one of Jeannie Dayton's five daughters moves into a new home, among her first questions is, "Where is your baking center going to be?"

"I go through the process of what they'll need and where it should be," says Dayton, co-owner of Pantry Secrets and mom to Mindy Spencer. "Just think, 'If I am going to make bread or cookies or cakes, where do I need all the stuff to be?'"

EVERYTHING IN ITS PLACE

Place your measuring spoons, cups, and mixing bowls in one area, Dayton suggests. Have the most frequently used ingredients in the vicinity too. If, like Dayton, your baking center is in a central island, you might keep your flour and sugar inside drawers underneath. Without an island, these ingredients may be best stowed in a top cupboard or in canisters on the countertop. "It is easier to bake when you know that everything is where you need it and that you can pull it together in a small window of time," Dayton says.

There is little incentive to make a homemade cake if you have to dig the ingredients out of a dark pantry or run downstairs to haul up five-gallon buckets of sugar and flour every single time.

One tip: make sure the containers you buy for storing these ingredients have an opening wide enough to pass a measuring cup through. Natalie got small canisters years ago for a wedding present only to discover they were virtually useless in the kitchen because she couldn't even fit a half-cup measure inside. We both love the look of flour and sugar stored in glass containers. We've bought ones with wide openings at Target for less than ten dollars each and love how they are both functional and beautiful in the kitchen.

REAL SIMPLE

Really, anything that simplifies the baking process will contribute to your success. Dayton's daughters are now grown, but when they were younger, constant interruptions during baking and cooking (or, really, any activity) were a way of life.

Trying to count out ten and a half cups while measuring flour for homemade bread was often tricky—the phone would ring, or a child would beckon, or a doorbell would chime. Guessing on the amount of flour already added wasn't a good idea, but neither was dumping out the flour and starting over. So Dayton sought out a cup that would hold the ten and a half cups of flour needed for her recipe. That way, the highest she would ever need to count to was one.

"Think about all the little baking tasks that you do over and over and over again," Dayton says. "If you can just chop off a few minutes of this or that, by streamlining or creating a system that works, it does make it easier."

A BIT OF THIS AND THAT

If there are certain recipes you make from scratch often, consider putting together your own premade mixes. Use heavy-duty ziplock bags to combine measured dry ingredients. Leave out yeast if the recipe calls for it. It is better added with the wet ingredients, such as eggs or oil, just before baking.

Use a permanent marker to write the date each mix was made and include instructions for baking. Premade mixes are ideal for waffles, pancakes, or muffins, as well as cookie or brownie recipes. Add a bow and a card, and you've got a thrifty gift too.

• PANTRY BASICS •

In case you haven't noticed a trend, let us point it out again. Baking is much easier when you are prepared. Here are basic ingredients that are helpful to have on hand—ideally stored in your baking center. Use as high of quality ingredients as you can reasonably afford. Figure out what generic products you like and, conversely, which ones you don't.

> **FLOUR**—There are different kinds of flour, including unbleached or bleached all-purpose flour, cake flour, pastry flour, and bread flour. All are ground from varieties of whole wheat, such as soft white or hard red. Hard wheat has a higher protein content than soft wheat. Why should you care? Because higher protein levels mean greater potential for gluten development. Gluten increases the elasticity and strength of baked goods. All-purpose flour is usually made from a blend of hard and soft wheat. If you're going to pick one flour to store, this is the one. Experiment with cake and pastry flours as you have

the time and money. There will likely be trial and error involved. For bread making, you'll want either 100-percent whole-wheat flour or bread flour on hand.

❧ SUGAR—Derived from sugar cane and beets, sugar isn't just for adding sweetness. It also adds color, volume, and texture. Granulated white sugar is the refined sugar called for in many recipes. Brown sugar is often used interchangeably. It is made by adding molasses to white sugar and comes in several colors, like light and dark. Confectioners' sugar is refined sugar ground to a powder (also called powdered sugar). It is commonly used in icings. Coarse sugar is typically used as a garnish.

❧ HONEY—Made by honeybees, this sticky sweetener can be substituted for granulated sugar in most recipes. Use less honey than sugar. For instance, if a recipe calls for ½ cup of sugar, use only ⅓ cup of honey.

❧ COCOA—Unsweetened cocoa is available in two types: natural and Dutch-processed. Dutch-processed cocoa has a milder flavor. Natural cocoa has a bitter, deep chocolate flavor. Sweetened cocoa has sugar added (and sometimes milk products too) and is mostly used in chocolate drink mixes.

❧ BAKING POWDER—This is a leavening agent used to cause batters to rise when baked. It should be stored in a cool, dry place and replaced every six to twelve months. To test baking powder for effectiveness, mix 1 teaspoon with ½ cup of hot water. The mixture should bubble immediately.

❧ BAKING SODA—Another leavening agent, baking soda is about four times as strong as baking powder. It is used in recipes that include an acidic ingredient, such as vinegar or buttermilk. Baking soda has a long shelf life when stored in a cool, dry place. To test baking soda for effectiveness, mix ¼ teaspoon with 2 teaspoons of vinegar and watch for immediate bubbles.

◈ **SALT**—Salt intensifies flavors and is crucial in baking. Regular iodized salt will do in most baking recipes. For cooking, many people prefer coarser sea salt or kosher salt.

◈ **YEAST**—This is a living organism used to leaven baked goods. The most common types are regular active dry yeast and rapid-rise or instant yeast. They are interchangeable, but keep in mind instant yeast requires half the rise time of regular active yeast.

◈ **BUTTER**—This fat comes in unsalted and salted versions. Choose unsalted butter when baking. (Most recipes assume this is the kind being used.) Alternatives are vegetable shortening or lard.

◈ **OIL**—Recipes for pancakes, waffles, and muffins often call for oil in place of butter. Canola oil is a good, heart-healthy option. We like to substitute applesauce for oil, one to one, for taste and caloric reasons.

◈ **MILK**—There are a quite a few kinds of milk used in baking—regular milk, buttermilk, powdered milk, evaporated milk, and sweetened condensed milk. They are not interchangeable, except when a recipe lists substitutions. For instance, you can usually swap 1 cup milk plus 1 tablespoon vinegar or lemon juice for buttermilk. Also, powdered milk can usually be reconstituted in various ways; read the side of your can for instructions. (Use the Internet if all else fails.) Unless a recipe instructs otherwise, use whole milk, not nonfat or 1 percent. Evaporated milk and sweetened condensed milk are shelf stable, so buy a few cans at a time.

◈ **CHOCOLATE**—Chocolate is chocolate, right? Wrong. There are decided differences between high-quality and grocery-store-quality chocolate, the main two of which are taste and price. The good news is, unless you have an extremely refined palette, you may have a hard time distinguishing among good, better, and best. Most of the world's chocolate beans come from the Ivory Coast in Africa. This means a lot of chocolate is quite similar. Fine chocolate manufacturers seek out exotic locales to harvest their beans. The results are distinct tastes and flavors. But unless you're producing high-end chocolates, a "better" quality chocolate is just fine. Perform an inexpensive taste test by buying a few bags of chocolate chips at the grocery store. (Tough job, right?) If you bake with a lot of chocolate, contact a baker's cash-and-carry or restaurant supply in your area to see if you can purchase a slab in bulk.

• SPICE GIRLS •

Spices are the life of the kitchen party, so to speak. They can wake up dull recipes in no time at all. Many of the spices you have in your cupboard are likely for savory uses. But there are sweet spices too. Heck, some can go either way.

We usually keep quantities of these around:

- CINNAMON—Sticks for stirring into hot chocolate; ground for adding to muffins or pancakes or for dusting on toast and apples.

- ALLSPICE—Dash on French toast or add to pie filling. Also works with ground beef in recipes like Swedish meatballs.

- CLOVES—Add to pumpkin pie. For a classic holiday ham, use cloves in your glaze.

- GINGER—Dried and ground from gingerroot, ginger adds zing to ham or pork recipe and is used for quintessential holiday recipes, like gingerbread cookies.

- PUMPKIN PIE SPICE—A blend of cinnamon, ginger, nutmeg, and allspice gives that classic pumpkin pie taste.

NUTMEG—Sprinkled over carrots or cookies, nutmeg is delicious. TV chefs often use a microplane to grate whole nutmeg right into sweet and savory dishes.

POPPY SEEDS—A star ingredient in yummy breads and muffins. Also often used for homemade salad dressings.

CREAM OF TARTAR—Helps keep egg whites stiff. Used in meringues, snickerdoodles, and angel food cake.

VANILLA EXTRACT—Probably one of the most popular flavors in baking. Pure vanilla extract is taken from vanilla bean pods. Imitation is, well, an imitated version. Most specialty grocers carry Mexican, Madagascar, and Tahitian vanilla.

ALMOND EXTRACT—Used most famously in macaroons.

• ALL INGREDIENTS ON DECK •

Before you launch into a recipe, make sure you have all the ingredients you need. If Natalie had a dime for every time she discovered she was missing an ingredient in the midst of baking, she'd be a rich woman. True, necessity is the mother of invention, but baking is a science, so most ingredients are quite crucial. Chocolate chip cookies aren't the same without chocolate chips. And forget about leaving out the butter.

• QUICK REVIEW •

Read through the recipe and familiarize yourself with the instructions. Although it may just sound like words on a page to you, each verb implies a specific action crucial to the success of a recipe.

For instance, many cookie recipes call for creaming together butter and sugar. This isn't fancy talk; creaming the ingredients introduces pockets of air into the batter. These bubbles improve the taste and texture of the finished product. Cheesecake recipes say to add the eggs one at a time. This reduces the likelihood of protein pockets and cracks in the finished product. Kneading bread for the specified amount of time ensures proper gluten development. Using butter at room temperature will create a far nicer finished product than using, say, melted or rock-hard butter.

Here is a short review of terms that will come in handy:

- ✍ **BATTER** (n.): A mixture of flour, liquid, and other ingredients thin enough to pour.

- ✍ **BEAT** (v.): To combine ingredients and incorporate air with a rapid circular motion. This can be done with a wooden spoon, whisk, electric hand mixer, or stand mixer.

- ✍ **BOIL** (v.): To heat a liquid until bubbles rise to the surface and break.

- ✍ **CREAM** (v.): To beat one or more ingredients, typically butter and sugar or butter, sugar, and eggs until the mixture is light and fluffy. As a noun, *cream* refers to heavy cream.

- ✍ **CRIMP** (v.): To seal the edges of two or more layers of dough using your fingertips or the tines of a fork.

- ✍ **COMBINE** (v.): To stir together two or more ingredients until well mixed.

- ✍ **CUT IN** (v.): To add fat (such as butter) to a dry ingredient. This is usually done with a fork or pastry blender. You can even do it with your fingers.

- ✍ **DASH** (n.): A very small amount of an ingredient thrown into a dish, generally less than $\frac{1}{8}$ of a teaspoon.

- ✍ **DOUGH** (n.): A soft mixture of flour, liquids, fat, and other ingredients. It should be solid enough to be manipulated by hand.

DRIZZLE (v.): To pour a liquid (such as melted chocolate) in a thin line over food.

DUST (v.): To sprinkle with sugar, flour, or cocoa.

FOLD (v.): To gently combine ingredients, often using a spatula. In this process, no air is removed.

• **GARNISH** (v.): To decorate using food.

GLAZE (v.): To coat with a thin, liquid icing before or after food is cooked.

GREASE (v.): To spread fat, such as oil or cooking spray, on the surface of a pan to prevent sticking.

GRIND (v.): To break down food into smaller particles by forcing it through a grinder.

KNEAD (v.): To make dough smooth and elastic by pressing or punching it with one's hands, or by using an electric dough mixer.

LUKEWARM (adj.): A temperature that is not hot or cold. Lukewarm should be about 105°F.

MIX (v.): To stir together ingredients until they are well combined. "Mix until just moistened" means that ingredients are wet but batter is still a bit lumpy.

PEAKS (n.): Refers to points developed in a batter, such as meringue, usually formed after beating with an electric mixer. "Soft peaks" are soft and rounded. "Stiff peaks" are stiff and hard.

PUREE (v.): To liquefy a solid using a blender or food processor.

RIND (n.): The skin of citrus fruit or cheese.

❧ ROLLING BOIL (n.): A type of boil so rapid that you can't stir it away.

❧ SCALD (v.): To heat a liquid to just below its boiling point. This word is also sometimes interchanged with blanch, which means to plunge rapidly in boiling water.

❧ SCORE (v.): To make shallow cuts on the surface of a food, using a knife. This can be done to enhance flavor or appearance, or both.

❧ SET (v.): To refrigerate until consistency thickens and becomes solid.

❧ SOFTENED (adj.): Butter, cream cheese, or the like in a soft enough state for blending, but not melted.

❧ STIR (v.): To combine with a spoon or whisk using a circular motion.

❧ WHIP (v.): To beat rapidly to incorporate air into a mixture to lighten and increase its volume.

❧ ZEST (n.): The outermost layer of citrus fruits. As a verb, zest means to remove this layer using a knife or citrus zester.

• MAKING BREAD •

Many seasoned bakers shy away from homemade bread, thinking it is simply too hard to get tasty, consistent results. Learn how to make goodies first, they say, and then try your hand at baking bread. We politely disagree.

Learning how to make your own bread is one of the biggest bangs for your baking bucks. It can save you a ton of money, even in just one year. Plus, mastering this oft-intimidating task will likely give you the confidence boost you need to confront more complicated recipes.

Dayton and Spencer, of Pantry Secrets, are well known for their incredibly simple and straightforward bread recipe. Sold on DVDs and taught at in-home classes, the Pantry Secrets method teaches novices and experts how to make homemade bread in one hour from start to finish for around twenty-five cents a loaf. (Even less if you grind your own wheat). You can learn more at pantrysecrets.net.

Elyssa and Natalie learned to make bread using Pantry Secrets's straightforward method and now confidently make bread using any recipe. The key to confidence is finding the right recipe to learn on. Ask family members to share their easy bread recipes with you, order an instructional DVD, or find an illustrated cookbook with step-by-step pictures. Better yet, recruit a bread-baking friend to show you how to make bread.

Here are a few time-tested bread making tips:

- **KEEP IT SIMPLE.** Start with a recipe that has simple ingredients and steps (see our favorite whole wheat recipe at the end of this chapter). Try to avoid recipes that require fancy ingredients you don't normally keep on hand or require multiple rises—you can tackle those recipes after you master basic bread making. Natalie learned to make regular white bread using bread flour first, then moved onto whole wheat bread made with freshly ground flour. Now, she isn't scared to make breads that rise several times, such as pita bread and naan.

- **LESS IS MORE.** Adding too much flour can result in a dry, tough end product. Most recipes give a range of flour required, say twelve to fourteen cups, so start by adding the lowest amount. Gradually add the rest of the flour, keeping in mind that you may not need to add it all. A good recipe will let you know what texture to watch for, and it is crucial to stop adding flour when that texture is reached. Add the necessary amount of flour before the kneading process. Never add flour to a recipe after kneading is done.

- **THE RIGHT STUFF.** Not all recipes call for the same texture in kneaded dough. Some recommend sticky dough, others call for dough that is slightly stiff. But as a general rule, you want dough to be more on the sticky side than not. This is where a class or one-on-one instruction from a friend is helpful— after you've felt the right dough texture, it is much easier to replicate. If the dough is difficult to handle after the kneading process, use a baking spray or flour to make it more manageable.

❧ **DON'T BE SCARED OF YEAST.** Most grocery stores sell several types of yeast, including dry active, quick-rise, bread machine, and instant yeast. Don't be scared by the varieties—the main difference is the names! Natalie has successfully substituted instant yeast in many recipes. She prefers to stock instant yeast because it doesn't require proofing in warm water like active dry yeast does. A quick word on water: If you are adding yeast directly to dry ingredients, hot tap water is okay to use. If you are using a yeast that must first be proofed, stick with lukewarm water and wait for it to bubble before mixing with other ingredients.

❧ **GET A RISE OUT OF IT.** Some recipes rise in a warm oven, others at room temperature on a countertop. Follow your recipe's instructions for rising, keeping in mind that you want to protect raised bread from drafts and, if raising on the counter, cover with a clean kitchen towel to keep it moist. Try not to jostle the bread after it has raised and carefully place it in the oven.

❧ **SHAPE MATTERS.** After going through the effort to make homemade bread, take a minute (literally) to nicely shape the loaves before placing in pans. Sure, you could just chuck it into a pan but folded ends and smooth tops make for a much nicer finished product.

❧ **DONE AND DONE.** There are lots of methods for determining whether a loaf of bread is done. The most reliable? Look for evenly browned tops and a browned bottom. A flick of the finger or tap on the bottom of a loaf should produce a hollow sound. After removing bread from the oven, let it cool for a few minutes, and then remove from pans. Let cool completely on a cooling rack so that air can circulate around the loaves. Setting a hot loaf directly on the countertop could result in a soggy bottom.

❧ **STORE AND SERVE.** Specialty kitchen stores sell good-quality bread bags for storage or you can purchase bread and food storage bags at most grocery stores. Thicker bags are best if you are planning to freeze loaves of bread—since most recipes make four or more loaves, Natalie often freezes at least two loaves per batch. To cut bread, we recommend a sharp serrated knife or, better yet, an electric knife. The latter is especially handy if you want to enjoy hot-from-the-oven bread without smashing the entire loaf.

• MAKING COOKIES •

One of Natalie's top ten baking catastrophes happened when she was a freshman at BYU and was making cookies for a friend at the Missionary Training Center. She couldn't figure out why the cookies were raw in the middle, even though she had gone way past the bake time on the recipe. Then she realized she had forgotten to separate the baking sheets, placing two, not one, in the oven.

Some baking mistakes are like that—simple human errors that can be easily fixed the next time. But other times, the outcome isn't what you'd hoped for. Maybe you wanted crunchy cookies, and yours came out soft. Or you wanted puffy, and the result was flat. What gives? Well, it comes down to science.

Here is a cheat sheet in case you've never set foot in a food science classroom:

- All-purpose flour is best for cookies. If you want denser cookies, use bread flour. If you prefer softer, use cake flour or pastry flour. Too much flour makes cookies dry, so we like to add a few tablespoons less than most recipes call for.

- If you want flatter cookies, use more baking soda. You can increase soda by up to a half without throwing off the flavor.

- Swap out eggs for milk to make cookies spread.

- Add more brown sugar (and less white) for crispier cookies.

- Use shortening instead of butter if you want softer cookies that won't spread too much.

- Chill dough in the refrigerator to make it easier to work with. This is a good idea when dough is too sticky to handle.

• SOME FOR NOW, FUN FOR LATER •

Because freshly baked cookies are too tasty to resist, we like to bake only a half batch at a time and freeze the rest of the dough for when another craving strikes. You can freeze cookies already dropped onto a baking sheet or freeze just the dough. For the latter, roll dough into a tube shape, cover with plastic wrap and then a layer or two of aluminum foil. To cook frozen cookies, add a few minutes to the bake time.

Speaking of bake time: Watch cookies closely beginning three minutes or so before the bake time is up. Snatch them out of the oven as soon as the edges start to brown, since they'll continue to bake after being removed from the oven.

• MAKING CAKES, BROWNIES, • AND OTHER GOODIES

It is simple to make cake and cakelike desserts from scratch. All you have to do is follow the "usual procedure." Cream together sugars and fats until light and fluffy. Add eggs to batter, one at a time, until thoroughly incorporated. Add additional liquid, such as milk or vanilla extract, mixing afterward. Combine dry ingredients in a separate bowl, sifting if the recipe advises. Add dry ingredients to wet ingredients a bit at a time. (Resist the urge to dump it all in at once.) Scrape down the sides of the bowl before each addition. Mix until just combined.

If you're making a double- or triple-layer cake, make sure to line bottoms of baking pans with parchment paper, even if you grease the pan. It's the best way to ensure you'll be able to get out each layer in one piece.

Tip: you can freeze individual pieces of cake just like you can cookies.

• MAKING PIES •

There is something innately comforting about a piece of pie. You really can't go wrong with a piece of apple or pecan pie, served with a scoop of vanilla ice cream. But getting to that oh-so-right finished product can be a bit tricky.

The main problem most people encounter with pies is the crust. (We're talking about a flaky pastry crust, not a graham cracker or chocolate cookie crust). It won't roll out. It falls apart. It burns. So Natalie asked her grandmother Rose Aldridge, a first-class pie maker,[3] for her no-fail tips:

- ✣ Use all-purpose flour. You can use fancy pastry flour if you have it in your pantry, but don't make a special trip to the store.

- ✣ Look for a recipe that uses shortening. This is best for a tender crust. You can use a mix of butter and shortening if you prefer the butter taste.

- ✣ Make sure ingredients are cold. Cold liquid, cold fat, never at room temperature.

- ✣ Don't use your hands to blend flour and fat. Instead, cut together gently with a pastry blender or even two knives. Do this until pea-sized pieces form. You want the butter and/or shortening to be visible.

- ✣ Form a ball with your pastry and roll out on a well-floured surface. You can use two pieces of waxed paper, if you want.

- ✣ Place an upside-down pie pan atop the pastry and trace with a knife, leaving room for fluting crust.

- ✣ Poke a few holes with a fork in the bottom and sides of the pastry before baking.

- ✛ Add a bit of sugar to pastry intended for fruit or nut pies. Sprinkling the crust with cinnamon sugar takes it over the top. Leave this out if you are making crusts for savory items like chicken pot pies, meat pies, or quiche.

- ✛ Watch for browning on the edges of the pie crust. If the color is coming on too quickly, place cut strips of aluminum foil around the crust. You could also buy a pie crust shield at a specialty store.

- ✛ If your pie crust falls apart despite all efforts, don't toss it and start over. Break it into small pieces and call it a crumble. Problem solved.

• PRESENTATION •

After slaving to make treats taste yummy, don't forget to make them look pretty too. Unless you have presentable bakeware that you plan to serve out of, line pans with parchment paper, leaving a few inches of hangover so you can pull cakes, squares, and such out of the pan. It is best to wait until the item has cooled, so this will require advance planning. Depending on if and how you plan to use icing, it may be best applied before removing the item from the pan.

Arrange portions on a platter so that no one has to fumble with a knife and fork. Those scenarios rarely end well for the dessert. Natalie prefers the crisp look

of white platters for serving. Elyssa likes antique-looking silver dishes.

If you're icing at this point, go ahead. Use water to clean up extra icing on cake stands or other serving pieces.

When you really want to impress people, garnish your goodies. You could use coarse or colored sugar, or zest if the food is fruity. One of Natalie's friends goes all out by topping cupcakes with a peek of what's inside. Her chocolate peanut butter cupcakes have a quarter peanut butter cup atop peanut butter buttercream icing. It's oh-so-delicious.

• RECIPES •

Just as in the cooking section, we've included some of our favorite recipes, this time for baked goods. Many are from friends and family members, and most are easy as, well, pie.

SIMPLE CHOCOLATE SAUCE

2 cups sugar

4 Tbsp. cocoa

1 (12-oz.) can evaporated milk

½ cup butter

Melt butter in medium saucepan. Add sugar, stirring to dissolve, then cocoa. Whisk in evaporated milk. Bring to a rolling boil, stirring, for 2 minutes. Let cool and serve over brownies, ice cream, or cake.

—*Courtesy Alyce Burt, Natalie's maternal grandmother*

ORANGE JUICE COOKIES

¾ cup shortening

1 cup sugar

2 eggs, beaten

½ tsp. baking soda

¼ tsp. salt

1 cup coconut

¾ cup orange juice

2½ cups flour, sifted

Cream shortening and sugar. Add well-beaten eggs to mixture. In a separate bowl, sift flour, salt, and baking soda. Add half of flour mixture, then half of orange juice. Mix well. Add remaining orange juice and remaining flour mixture. Add coconut. Bake at 400°F for about 10 minutes.

—Courtesy Genevieve Christensen, Elyssa's maternal great-grandmother. Genevieve was such a prolific cookie baker that her grandchildren and great-grandchildren actually called her "Grandma Cookie" throughout her life.

CHOCOLATE PEANUT BUTTER CHIP COOKIES

1 cup shortening
  (or ½ cup butter and ½ cup shortening)

1½ cups sugar

2 eggs

2 tsp. vanilla

2 cups flour

⅔ cup cocoa

¾ tsp. baking soda

⅛ tsp. salt

2 cups peanut butter chips

Cream together shortening and sugar. Add eggs and vanilla with usual procedure. Mix dry ingredients separately, and then add to wet ingredients a third at a time. Add peanut butter chips and mix to distribute. Drop by teaspoonfuls onto ungreased baking sheet. Bake at 350°F for 8 to 10 minutes. Remove from oven when centers are still glistening slightly. Cool completely on rack.

OATMEAL COOKIES

3 eggs, well beaten	2½ cups flour
1 cup raisins	1 tsp. salt
1 tsp. vanilla	2 tsp. baking soda
1 cup shortening	1 tsp. cinnamon
1 cup brown sugar	2 cups quick oatmeal
1 cup granulated sugar	½ cup chopped walnuts

Combine eggs, raisins, and vanilla. Let mixture stand for 1 hour. Thoroughly cream together shortening and brown and white sugars. Sift flour, salt, soda, and cinnamon into sugar mixture. Mix well. Blend in eggs, raisins, oatmeal, and nuts. (Dough will be stiff.)

Put heaping teaspoonfuls of dough onto ungreased cookie sheet or roll into small balls and flatten. Bake in 350-degree oven 10–12 minutes, or until lightly brown. Do not overbake.

—*Courtesy Genevieve Christensen*

MOM'S BROWNIES

½ cup butter or margarine	2 eggs
1 cup sugar	4 Tbsp. unsweetened cocoa powder
1 tsp. vanilla	¾ cup flour

Melt butter and cream with sugar. Add vanilla and eggs following usual procedure. Mix in cocoa and flour. Coat an 8-inch square pan with cooking spray. Pour in batter. Bake at 350°F for 25 minutes, or until toothpick inserted in center comes out clean. Variations: Sprinkle chocolate chips or nuts over batter before cooking.

—*Courtesy Shelley Aldridge, Natalie's mother*

CHOCOLATE MOUSSE PIE

1 chocolate sandwich cookie pie crust

2 (7-ounce) giant milk chocolate bars

1 (12-ounce) container frozen whipped topping, defrosted

small chocolate bar for chocolate shavings

Break chocolate up into small pieces and microwave in a microwave-safe bowl for 30 seconds. Remove and stir. Continue microwaving at 30-second intervals and then stirring until chocolate is melted and smooth. Add defrosted frozen whipped topping and mix with chocolate. Batter should reach an even, creamy consistency. Pour into chocolate sandwich cookie crust, then garnish with chocolate shavings. (You can make these with a knife or potato peeler.) Refrigerate several hours until pie filling is firm. Serve chilled.

—*Courtesy Kathy Madsen, Elyssa's mom*

CHERRY-ALMOND BUTTERCREAM ICING

½ cup unsalted butter

½ cup shortening

⅛ tsp. salt

5 cups powdered sugar

¼ cup plus 1 Tbsp. milk

2 tsp. cherry extract

2 tsp. almond extract

Soften butter in microwave 15 seconds, then cream with shortening. Add salt. Add sugar one cup at a time. Mix well after each cup on medium speed, scraping the sides and bottom. Add milk and beat at high speed until fluffy. Add cherry and almond extracts and beat at medium speed. You may need to add a bit more to taste, depending on how strong you like the flavoring. *Note that you can switch out the cherry and almond flavorings for vanilla, lemon, or even orange flavoring, depending on your needs. Start with a tablespoon of flavoring, and add more to taste.

APPLE CRISP

7 Jonagold apples, cored and sliced

¼ cup sugar

1 Tbsp. lemon juice

Oatmeal Topping:

1 cup flour

½ cup old-fashioned rolled oats

⅓ cup sugar

⅓ cup brown sugar

½ tsp. cinnamon

½ cup cold butter,
  cut into ¼-inch pieces

1 tsp. salt

Heat oven to 375°F. Generously grease with butter a 9-inch by 13-inch pan. Sprinkle apples with lemon juice. Place apples in pan then add sugar, then topping.

To make topping: Combine flour, oats, sugar, brown sugar, cinnamon, and salt in a large mixing bowl. Add the butter pieces and use your fingers to cut in the butter until you have pea-sized crumbs. Spread the topping evenly over the apples and press it down gently with your palm. Bake for 45 minutes until golden brown.

—*Courtesy MaryAnn Andrus, Elyssa's mother-in-law*

AUNT MELODY'S BROWN SUGAR TOPPING

1 cup heavy whipping cream

1 cup packed brown sugar

Combine ingredients in a bowl. Cover and refrigerate at least six hours or overnight. Whip with electric mixer until thickened. Use as frosting on angel food cake.

—*Courtesy Melody Baxter, Natalie's aunt*

CARROT CAKE

4 eggs

2 cups sugar

1½ cups melted shortening

2 tsp. baking soda

1 tsp. salt

3 tsp. cinnamon

2 cups flour

½ cup walnuts, chopped

½ cup raisins

3 cups finely grated carrots

Cream cheese frosting:

1 (8-oz.) package cream cheese, softened to room temperature

2½ cups powdered sugar

3 Tbsp. butter, softened

½ tsp. vanilla

Beat eggs in mixer (or in mixing bowl with whisk). Add shortening and sugar, beating to incorporate. Add soda, salt, cinnamon, and flour. Mix to incorporate. Stir in walnuts, raisins, and carrots. Pour into two greased 9-inch cake pans or a 9-inch by 13-inch baking dish. Bake at 350°F for 40 to 45 minutes. Cool on rack. To make frosting, beat cream cheese and butter together in a medium mixing bowl. Add powdered sugar in three additions. Stir in vanilla.

—Courtesy Shelley Aldridge

WHOLE WHEAT BREAD

7 cups plus 5 cups whole wheat flour

  (grind your own if you have a wheat grinder)

$^2/_3$ cups vital wheat gluten

2½ Tbsp. instant yeast

5 cups hot water

2 Tbsp. salt

$^2/_3$ cup oil

$^2/_3$ cup honey

2½ Tbsp. bottled lemon juice

    Mix seven cups of flour, vital wheat gluten, and yeast in mixer with dough hook. Add the water and mix for one minute. Cover and let rest for 10 minutes. (This is called sponging and the dough should rise slightly during this time). Add salt, oil, honey and lemon juice and mix for one minute. One cup at a time and beating between each addition, mix in last five cups of flour. Knead for 10 minutes until dough pulls away from the sides of the bowl but is still soft.

    Preheat oven to 350°F for one minute then turn off. Turn kneaded dough onto an oiled countertop. Divide into four loaves, shape and placed into greased bread pans. Place in warm oven and let rise for 10 to 15 minutes, until the dough reaches the top of the pan. Keep dough in oven, turn oven to 350°F and bake for 30 minutes. Remove from oven and let rest three minutes. Turn bread from pans onto cooling rack and cool completely before storing.

—Adapted from a recipe from dealstomeals.blogspot.com.

SQUIRRELED AWAY
Fun With Food Storage

Elyssa and her sister Emmalie were talking food storage the other day. Emmalie said she just wanted to get a year's supply of wheat, sugar, and oil she could stick in the basement for thirty years. She wouldn't worry about it ever again, knowing it was there if she needed it. Never mind that she didn't know what to do with wheat. She'd be comforted just knowing it was there.

It's tempting to think of food storage this way—as tons and tons of wheat and sugar to be kept in some dark corner for decades, to be addressed only when it's about to go bad or the sky is falling. But doing so really misses out on one of the greatest advantages of food storage. Extra supplies will definitely help you in an emergency or job loss, but food storage is also a simple way to stretch your grocery dollar. It's a way to augment your day-to-day food supply with items purchased in bulk at rock-bottom prices.

You don't want to store a year's worth of food until it goes bad—think of the money you'd be throwing away! Instead, you want to stockpile nonperishable items your family regularly consumes, when you can get them at the best prices.

Perhaps in part because the idea of amassing an entire year's supply of food was overwhelming to many members, the LDS Church has in the past few years modified its guidelines on food storage. The Church now recommends that members store water and a three-month supply of food they regularly eat, and then work on long-term storage. The Church also counsels to build up a financial reserve, something you are hopefully motivated to work on after reading this book's section on family finances.

In a 2007 pamphlet *All Is Safely Gathered In: Family Home Storage*, the First Presidency of The Church of Jesus Christ of Latter-day Saints urges moderation in food storage. "We ask that you be wise as you store food and water and build your savings. Do not go to extremes; it is not prudent, for example, to go into debt to establish your food storage all at once. With careful planning, you can, over time, establish a home storage supply and a financial reserve."[1]

In this statement, the words "over time" stand out. You don't have to outlay hundreds of dollars up-front for food storage. In fact, it's probably best to set a small budget—say, ten to fifty dollars of the grocery bill each week, even five dollars if that's all you can afford—and use that money to purchase the best deals on nonperishable items you can find.

• IT'S UP TO YOU •

If you've read the money management chapter, you may notice a theme. And there definitely is one. Part of being a good homemaker and living providently is being self-reliant. Now is the time to prepare so that in an emergency or financial hardship, you don't want to have to rely on your parents, your neighbors, your church, or the government to rescue you. "Some people think that if there is a disaster in the world, the Church is going to take care of them or the government or their neighbor," says Jeannie Dayton, co-owner of Pantry Secrets. "But what will you tell your kids if you aren't prepared, and they are hungry?"[2]

Maybe you aren't even married yet and worrying about hungry kids seems like a long way off. It may be, but the younger you are when you start thinking about saving a little extra food and money, the easier it will be down the road.

• On Your Mark, Get Set, Store! •

So where should you get started? With water, says Don Pectol, vice president of customer service for the Utah-based retailer Emergency Essentials. "In terms of your storage plan, the number one thing is water," he says. "A person can live up to a month without food, but within days, you may have damage to vital organs without water."[3]

How much water do you need to store? The Federal Emergency Management Agency recommends storing at least a three-day supply of water per person. Households should store a minimum of one gallon of water per person per day. "A normally active person needs at least one gallon of water daily just for drinking," says the agency on its website, www.fema.gov.[4]

Additionally, there are factors that may increase the need for water, says FEMA. Children, nursing mothers, and those who are sick will need more water. A medical emergency may require the use of more water, and a very hot climate could double the amount of water needed.

A three-day supply of drinking water is the minimum you should store, of course. It's ideal to store more if you can. Pectol of Emergency Essentials recommends storing a two-week supply of water for each person in your household (one gallon per day). So does Shandra Madsen, owner of Deals to Meals, a Utah-based company that helps people build up their food storage.[5]

• How to Store It •

FEMA recommends purchasing commercially bottled water and storing it in its original containers, observing the expiration date listed on the packaging. This is an easy but expensive option. If you want to prepare your own storage containers, FEMA recommends purchasing food-grade water storage containers from a camping or surplus supply stores. (These are also available at retailers such as Emergency Essentials and Macey's Food & Drug in Utah, and occasionally at Walmart. You can also order online from Emergency Essentials at beprepared .com.) These containers should be thoroughly cleaned and rinsed, according to FEMA, and filled according to the directions. The website also gives directions for storing water in two-liter soda bottles, a cheaper option than commercially bottled water or food-grade storage containers. For information on storing in two-liter soda bottles, visit http://www.ready.gov/water.

If you are adding water to a food-grade container yourself and have access to chlorinated municipal water, you will want to use a clean, food-grade hose to fill the container. Additional purification is not necessary because it should already be free of microorganisms, says Pectol of Emergency Essentials.

If you are using untreated water, such as well water, you'll need to add "two drops of non-scented liquid household chlorine," to the water, according to the FEMA website. Make sure to tightly seal the container with its original lid (Don't touch the insides, explains FEMA, because this will contaminate it). The agency says that non-commercially treated water should be restocked every six months.

The LDS Church also has water storage and purification guidelines on its Provident Living website, www.providentliving.org.

Water should be stored in a cool place with a consistent temperature, says Pectol. Basements are an ideal area for storage, but you can use your garage if you need to (make sure the containers are raised off of the cement so the water doesn't take on a bad flavor).

Also keep some water in small, portable containers near an exit to your house to grab in case of an emergency. (Elyssa and Natalie both keep several gallons of water in the back of their minivans, where it's readily accessible should they need to drive off with it, or should they need it while driving.)

• A Three-Month Supply of Food •

In its 2007 *All Is Safely Gathered In: Family Home Storage* pamphlet, the LDS Church says the following about a three-month supply of food:

"Build a small supply of food that is part of your normal, daily diet. One way to do this is to purchase a few extra items each week to build a one-week supply of food. Then you can gradually increase your supply until it is sufficient for three months. These items should be rotated regularly to avoid spoilage."[6]

No matter what stage of life you are in, you probably have a pretty good idea of what you like to eat. The trick is to just keep a little extra of it on hand. The following suggestions will help you save money while you are acquiring it.

• First Things First •

Make a list. You may find it helpful to make a list of a handful of favorite family meals and all of the ingredients that go into them. That way, you will know what to sales to watch for at the grocery store. If, say, your family likes a lot of Mexican food, you can look for sales in the Hispanic foods aisles for sales on chiles, salsa, beans, sauces, and so forth.

Shandra Madsen of Deals to Meals takes it a step further and recommends starting off with purchasing in bulk enough to make one breakfast, one lunch, and one dinner that your family regularly eats. She says it's important to buy all of the items that would go in this meal. (If your family eats cereal for breakfast, for example, you need to stock up on a three-month supply of cereal and of powdered milk.) Once you have purchased a three-month supply of each one breakfast, lunch and dinner, you can pick another daylong menu and start to work on it, she says.

⚘ *Watch and record prices.* Keep your list in a notebook and record the ingredients' regular prices at the grocery store where you shop. Then watch coupons and ad circulars for items to go on sale. Remember, if you don't want to buy one can of peaches at full retail price, you most certainly don't want to buy twenty. Some people find it worth it to sign up for a couponing service (typically through a newspaper and free) or a subscription website (such as Madsen's www.dealstomeals.com) that will alert you to store sales and promotions.

⚘ *Don't break the bank.* Set an amount for food storage in your grocery budget and stick to it. At first, it may only be ten or twenty dollars. Use that money to buy in bulk the best deals you can find on non-perishable items. And then use them! It's so much better to pay forty cents for a can of beans than one dollar. As you build your pantry, you'll hopefully get to the point where you are buying the majority of nonperishable items at their lowest prices. Because you will already have a supply of items you commonly use on hand, your weekly grocery bill should decrease. This extra money can then go toward more food storage items. It's a positive cycle.

⚘ *Think about meat.* Remember you can stockpile meat when it goes on sale as well. Meat is typically the most expensive item in any meal, so taking advantage of a good meat sale means extra savings. If space permits, it's helpful to have an extra chest or freestanding freezer in your home for storage, says Madsen of Deals to Meals. If that's not possible, purchase as much meat as you can store and afford. To prevent freezer burn, items in the freezer need at least two layers. For example, chicken breasts purchased in a family pack can be split for individual servings, wrapped in plastic wrap, and then sealed inside a ziplock bag.

- *Rotate, rotate, rotate.* To keep items from going bad, start using them immediately. When you put items away, put the newest items at the back of the pantry so that older items get used up first. It's also helpful to write the purchase date on everything you store.

- *Case lot sales!* In Utah, many grocery stores hold case lot sales, where they sell units of food by the case. These are often offered at deeply discounted prices, and it's a great way to quickly build your pantry. Even if you can only afford one case of food—typically between ten and thirty dollars—it's a great way to get started. Check with grocery stores in your area to see if they have similar practices. You can also purchase cases of food (and other bulk products) at membership warehouses such as Costco and Sam's Club.

- *Speaking of warehouses. . .* Membership warehouses can be a great place to stock up on quality food in bulk. But before you buy, make sure to compare the price to your local grocery store. Something's not automatically cheaper just because it's sold in bulk at a warehouse. Madsen says that condiments and spices are great deals at warehouses because they are bought in bulk. Most other items, she says, will eventually go on sale at a grocery store for a lower price.

- *Store to serve.* As a member of The Church of Jesus Christ of Latter-day Saints, you may have the opportunity to provide service by bringing a meal to someone in your ward or community. In fact, you may have the opportunity to do so frequently. Storing items for these meals will allow you to be ready to serve at a moment's notice, and it will reduce the cost of providing a meal to someone. Jeannie Dayton, of Pantry Secrets, says she keeps "brown bag" meals in her pantry with all the items she would need for something like a soup or casserole. These supplies are ready to go as soon as they are needed.

In addition to food items, remember to stockpile nonperishable items such as toilet paper, laundry detergent, soap, and shampoo.

• LONGER-TERM SUPPLY •

Once you've got the basics down, you can store additional items that have a long shelf life. On its Provident Living website, the LDS Church recommends storing grains such as wheat, white rice, and dried beans, which can last thirty years or more (at least to sustain life). It's recommended to store twenty-five pounds of grains per month and/or five pounds of dried beans per adult per month. "You may also want to add other items to your longer-term storage such as sugar, nonfat dry milk, salt, baking soda, and cooking oil. To meet nutritional needs, also store foods containing Vitamin C and other essential nutrients."[7]

Don Pectol of Emergency Essentials has another great idea for long-term food storage: garden seeds. "If I had to walk out the door with one can and only one can, I would get a can of garden seeds," he said. "You can count the number of seeds in an apple, but you cannot count the number of apples in a seed." Seeds are open pollinators, which means you can allow some plants to "seed" and collect for next year's planting.

Although no one has suggested it yet, Elyssa has a friend who keeps M&Ms in her food storage. She figures it's something she'll always need in abundant supply. Seeds and M&Ms aside, the cheapest place to buy these longer-term items is often a Latter-day Saint dry-pack cannery, now called home storage centers, says Madsen of Deals to Meals. Here you can buy everything from black beans to dried milk, from apple slices to pancake mix. Home storage center order forms are available online at www.providentliving.org.

And while building a long-term supply is an important food storage goal, remember it's not meant to be shoved in the basement and never used. You need to regularly cook with your long-term storage items. This helps your body adjust to whole grains, and if you ever need to use them in an emergency, you will already know how to do so.

If you are storing wheat, you'll want to invest in a wheat grinder to turn the wheat into flour for bread, pancakes, tortillas, and other baked items. You can purchase either a hand grinder or an electric grinder. A hand-crank grinder is handy (so to speak) in the event of a power loss. Basic versions, like Back-to-Basics brand, are available online at Amazon.com and at retailers nationwide, including Walmart, for around sixty dollars.

If you are going to make bread regularly, you'll love the convenience of an electric wheat grinder. These are available at kitchen and bread retailers, emergency retailers, and occasionally grocery stores with food storage sections. Electric grinders can cost one to three hundred dollars or more but are a worthwhile and necessary investment if you regularly make bread or store wheat. Natalie stubbornly, and unwisely, refused to store wheat until she bought a good-quality wheat grinder. But now she has a NutriMill and uses wheat so often that she stores more than the recommended amount.

Making homemade bread and pancakes or salad dressing from scratch doesn't take that much extra time, but it does take practice, says Shandra Madsen of Deals to Meals. "It's just a lifestyle," she says. And a healthy one too, because you are cooking with whole grains instead of processed white flour.

"It's just a part of life that can really be enjoyable, it can bring peace of mind to families," she says. "A lot of people think it's something their grandparents did, but that they don't need to do."

They are wrong, says Madsen. And at a basic level: "It's fun. It's fun to cook when you have food storage."

• WHERE TO PUT ALL OF THIS •

Don Pectol of Emergency Essentials says that food should be stored in a room with the coolest, steadiest temperatures in your home. While basements are an ideal place for storage, students in small apartments can find creative places for food storage. If you are cramped on living space, Pectol recommends storing food in appropriate containers under your bed. Bedrooms are typically kept at steady, moderate temperatures.

Low-moisture foods should be stored in sealed, air-tight containers to keep out moisture, insects, and oxygen, which can deteriorate food. The LDS Church recommends keeping longer-term storage in No. 10 cans, foil pouches, or PETE (polyethylene terephthalate) plastic bottles, all used with oxygen absorber packets.[8] This will preserve quality and keep foods safe from bugs. You can purchase No. 10 cans through home storage centers, foil pouches through Church Distribution Centers, and oxygen absorber packets from both places. In some conditions, you can also store dried foods in food-grade plastic buckets. These buckets need to have gaskets in the lid seals, and items should be treated with dry ice before being stored in this manner, according to the Church's website. (See www.providentliving.org for more information.

Jeannie Dayton of Pantry Secrets suggests storing your longer-term storage in a variety of ways. "Just like the saying, 'Don't put all your eggs on one basket,' don't store all your food the same way," she says. In a flood, No. 10 cans could be damaged. And rodents could potentially eat through foil packages. If one of these things were to happen to your storage, you wouldn't lose everything in its entirety, says Dayton. So she recommends storing the bulk of your food in a way that works best for you but having additional storage in other types of containers.

• 72-HOUR KITS •

One of the quickest, easiest, cheapest, and most important things you can do to prepare yourself for an emergency is to assemble a 72-hour kit. These portable kits are meant to contain the most basic essentials to sustain life for the first few days of an emergency. They should be kept in an easy-to-access space close to an exit of your house so that you can grab them in an emergency. Prepare one for each member of your family and include the basics: cash, nonperishable, high-energy food, as much water as you can fit and carry, vital medicines, copies of important documents such as birth certificates, personal sanitation items, and a light source. Keep the latter at the top of your kit in the event you lose power. Other items to consider, according to the Utah-based preparedness retailer Emergency Essentials, are something for shelter or warmth tools, first-aid items, communications items (such as a radio with batteries), extra clothing, and stress-relieving items.

Remember you'll occasionally need to go through these kits and determine if the items still fit the needs of your family. We like to go through ours every six months, in between the Saturday sessions of the LDS Church's general conference. When you periodically assess these kits, make sure to check the expiration date on any food and water they might contain. If any product is close to expiration, replace it or use it quickly.

In addition to these kits, store an additional portable supply of water close to an exit. That way, you can put it in a car should you need to quickly evacuate your house.

HOW DOES YOUR GARDEN GROW?

Whether your thumbs are black or green, you probably see the wisdom in growing a garden. Green in the truest sense, growing your own fruits and vegetables is a great way to reduce your carbon footprint and control where your food comes from. If you're concerned about pesticides and other chemicals on food, raising fruits and vegetables yourself is the surest way of knowing exactly what has been put on your food. Gardening also fosters self-reliance and hard work and can be great exercise. And you'll likely end up saving money.

On the LDS Church's Provident Living website, members are counseled that "Planting a garden, even a small one, allows for a greater degree of self-reliance. With the right information and a little practice, individuals and entire families can enjoy the many benefits of planting and tending a garden."[1]

If you've never planted a single seed, the thought of starting from scratch may make you want to dig a deep hole and climb in. So we asked Larry Sagers,[2] a noted horticulturist, about vegetable gardening for dummies. Sagers is a horticulturist specialist for the Utah State Extension Service at Thanksgiving Point in Lehi, Utah. He has written a gardening column for one of Utah's largest newspapers for more than fifteen years and cohosted a radio show on the subject for two decades. He and his wife also host garden tours across the country. Here, Sagers tells us where to begin.

• HIT PAY DIRT •

Unless it contains the right nutrients, your soil may be as worthless as, well, dirt. No amount of effort on your behalf, including hours spent staking, mulching, feeding, and watering, will help if you haven't properly prepped your soil.

In order for a plant to grow, it needs a combination of non-mineral and mineral elements. Non-mineral elements, such as hydrogen, carbon, and oxygen, are found in water and air. Mineral elements, such as nitrogen, phosphorus, and potassium, come from the soil, are dissolved in water, and absorbed through plant roots. However, these nutrients are not always available.

Lacking a degree in horticulture or botany, you may have a hard time determining what kind of soil you have and what it lacks. That is why it is so important to have an expert assess your soil before you lay a single seed down, Sagers says.

"Most people typically starting out are going to need to make improvements to their soil," Sagers says. "Depending on where you live, the soil will have different challenges."

• TESTING, TESTING 1-2-3 •

A professional soil test will give you an idea of what you're working with. These tests are performed at most Cooperative Extension System offices nationwide and should cost less than twenty dollars. These offices are a nationwide, non-credit educational network run by the United States Department of Agriculture's National Institute of Food and Agriculture. Each US state and territory has a central office at its land-grant university and a network of local or regional offices staffed by experts in various fields of research.

A routine test typically assesses the pH, salinity, texture, potassium, and phosphorus of soil. Such factors are important considerations when selecting plants, since most have a preference for alkaline or acidic soil and may have special nutrient requirements. For instance, if you have a very alkaline soil—like much of the soil in Utah, where we live—certain plants like blueberries will never grow well. If you live in the Northwest, where soil tends to be acidic, blueberries will do fine, Sagers says.

The texture of your soil—how much sand, clay, or silt it has—is another factor that affects the growth of plants. A soil test should include this information, or you can perform the National Gardening Association's ribbon test to get a general idea of texture. For the test, take a handful of moist soil and roll it between your palms until it forms a ribbon. If it feels gritty and breaks apart immediately, the soil is mainly sand. If the soil feels smooth and holds its shape for a short time before breaking apart, it's mostly silt. However, if it feels sticky and holds together in a ribbon, then it's clay.

• COMPOSTING 101 •

Once you know your dirt, you'll be more apt to decide how to improve the soil and what to plant. Organic matter is often the prescribed remedy, and composting is one of the thriftiest ways to access it. Composting is the decomposition of organic materials by microorganisms in a controlled environment. Or, in layman's terms, it's a big pile of rotting leaves, vegetable and fruit peels, and the like, that break down to create really nutritious soil.

You'll need a large amount of compost to fix soil. "You need at least five bushels of something to really make composting work," Sagers said. "Unless you have a lot of leaves you can use in the fall, you may not generate enough compost to fix your soil."

However, he says it is still worthwhile to compost, even if it takes a while to boost your stash. Many stores sell compost containers, but Sagers says a simple method for beginners is trench composting. The concept is simple: you dig a trench about a foot deep (any shape will do), add compost materials and bury it with the soil you dug out. That's it. The only way to mess it up is to add the wrong materials, namely meats, bones, dairy products, synthetic products, plastics, or pet wastes. Grass clippings, leaves or weeds, manures, fruits, vegetables, bark, and the like are all fair game.

• HERE COMES THE SUN •

Another consideration that will greatly impact the success of your garden is the amount of sun it receives. "Almost all vegetables have to grow with full sun," Sagers said. "That is at least six hours of direct sunlight every day."

It's a good idea to plant (or relocate) your garden to a sunny spot. If, like Natalie, your backyard (or balcony or patio) doesn't get full sun, you'll need to focus on growing leafy vegetables that don't produce a fruit, he says, like spinach or lettuce.

Or maybe like Elyssa, you have only a small area of your yard that gets full sun. In that case, you could try container gardening in the sunniest spots, or use a grow box or square-foot gardening method to pack a lot of punch into a small space. "You can grow a single tomato in a pot and have tomatoes pretty much all summer long off that," Sagers said. Your local library should have books on both kinds of gardening, and there is a plethora of information on the approaches on the Internet too.

• WATER WORLD •

All vegetables need water to grow. While you can definitely use a watering can, the easiest way to make sure plants are watered is to use an irrigation system, Sagers says. "Some plants need to be watered once or twice a day, and you may not be around to do that," he says. "When vegetables are stressed for water, they become tough, and the flavor goes out of them."

A simple drip irrigation system is fairly inexpensive and easy to install. Plus, such systems typically require less water than regular watering, so they're earth-friendly too.

The type of soil you have is also a factor in how often plants will need to be watered. If you have heavy clay soil, for instance, water will be more readily retained, and you won't need to water as frequently. If you're using a grow box with soil that was brought in, water will drain more rapidly and require watering more often, Sagers says. Again, that soil test will come in handy.

⋅ WHAT DOES YOUR GARDEN GROW? ⋅

Now comes a common question—What should I plant? Sagers answers that question with a query of his own: "What do you like to eat?"

"Too many people grow stuff because they hear that this is what people should grow," he said. "Or they just grab whatever they find in the nursery. If you're not going to eat it, don't bother to grow it."

It seems like a no-brainer, but you'd be surprised at how many people grow, say, radishes or beets or zucchini, without really having a hankering for them—or an idea of how to properly prepare them. "You need to look at what you eat at home and start with that," he says.

Narrow those favorites down by looking at what is easiest to grow. "There is a reason why tomatoes are the most popular vegetable in the United States," Sagers says, "and that is because they are easy to grow."

And because a good-sized tomato plant will yield around twenty pounds of fruit per season, it is a nice return on investment. Compare that with a corn plant that may take up the same amount of room as a tomato plant, but only yield one or two ears of corn. "From an economic standpoint, you want to grow things that give you the most return," Sagers said. "If you don't have a lot of space, let farmers grow the potatoes and corn and other things that take a lot of space, and you concentrate on things that are easier to grow and will give more yield."

Herbs like cilantro, parsley, oregano, and basil are easy to grow and use in the kitchen. Even if you lack the space or sunlight for a full-scale garden, herbs can be grown in small pots on a windowsill or patio.

• TIME AFTER TIME •

Consider the time it takes to harvest a crop when deciding how much to plant. For example, aside from the time it takes to grow fresh peas, you must also pick the peas, shell the peas, and then process them (cook them, prep them for freezing, or can them). Because frozen peas can be found inexpensively at any grocery store, it may be a good idea to just grow enough peas to eat fresh and forget about putting any up, Sagers says.

Look closely at a plant's projected output before sowing a plethora of seeds. Unless you really like zucchini.

Other considerations: regional crop diseases or common infestations, like Japanese Beetles or nematodes. Ask around at a nursery or contact a master gardener in your area to check for any habitual blight.

And, finally, make sure you're planting in the right season. Some regions, like the Mountain West, plant from spring to summer. Other areas, such as the South, have long growing seasons that spill into the fall and even winter.

• WEED WATCH •

Keeping weeds at bay will likely be one of your main challenges as a gardener. "Weeds, by all odds, are the most serious pests that you have in your vegetable garden," Sagers said. Unlike pests that are attracted to specific crops, such as hornworms on tomatoes, weeds don't care what you're growing. If left unchecked, they can completely take over a garden. "So you may plant and do all this work and end up with a very small crop or a very low-quality crop because the weeds have taken the nutrients and sunlight and water," he says.

For annual weeds, mechanical control is by far the best way to get rid of pesky growths. You can pull them, hoe them, or put mulch over them. However, when you have deep-rooted weeds that are spreading, you may need to use an herbicide, Sagers says. A good way to tell the difference between the weeds—without pulling up an entire segment of your garden—is to cut the tops off them. If they're lacking an elaborate root system, the tops of the weeds will die.

• SHARPEST TOOLS IN THE SHED •

There are dozens of gardening tools on the market, but it is best to start with the basics and add to your collection when you see a need. Also, if you're trying your hand at container gardening or square-foot gardening, a few of the most basic tools may be unnecessary. (Consult manuals specific to those methods for more details.) These tools are also handy for general yard maintenance:

- HAND TROWEL—for planting, weeding, and patting soil (Choose one that is sturdy and has a comfortable grip.)
- SPADE—for digging up dirt and plants
- GARDEN RAKE—with metal teeth, for working through soil
- HOE—to create trenches for seeds and bulbs
- LAWN RAKE—with large teeth to gather leaves and dead plants
- PRUNING SHEARS—for trimming branches and offshoots
- KNIFE—for harvesting and other miscellaneous tasks
- HOSE OR WATERING CAN—for watering plants

• STORING SEEDS •

Storing vegetable seeds for unforeseen emergencies isn't a bad idea. But if you want to be successful, you'll need to store the seeds properly.

To preserve seeds the longest, use cool temperatures and low humidity. Several companies market vacuum-packed seeds in No. 10 cans or pouches with shelf lives upward of twenty years. However, experts recommend using seeds well before that time is up.

Some gardeners harvest their own seeds from garden plants. But seeds are so easily and inexpensively obtained at the store that this isn't necessary.

• PUTTING UP FOOD •

You've planted a garden and reaped a plentiful harvest. Now, what are you going to do with all the food? Why, preserve it, of course.

For a time, canning, dehydrating, and other preservation methods were passé. But these old-school methods are gaining steam with a new generation of up-and-coming gardeners and cooks.

"Food preservation was starting to become a lost art," said Kathleen Riggs, family and consumer sciences agent with Utah State University Extension Office in Cedar City, Utah. "But a new crowd of young people are starting to do it."[3]

Riggs has worked for the USU Cooperative Extension Office for nearly thirty years. She says interest in food preservation usually piques from a desire to be more self-reliant. It is more prevalent in suburban and rural areas, typically because food preservation is linked with gardening, and urban areas just don't have the space.

"Many people like to grow their own produce and preserve that," Riggs says. Even if you don't have your own garden, preserving produce bought at local farm or market gives you more control over what you eat, she says. You know where it is from, how it was made, and often you can even control the level of sugar or other sweeteners.

According to the National Center for Home Food Preservation at the University of Georgia in Atlanta, there are more than a few tried-and-true food preservation methods: canning, freezing, drying, curing, smoking, fermenting, pickling, and making jams and jellies.

Each method has its merits, but canning and freezing are among the most popular. And no, using a pressure cooker or water-bath canner isn't as hard as it looks. "It's really not complicated," Riggs says. "You just have to follow instructions."

Although there are multiple ways to put up food, for the sake of brevity we'll cover only the most common methods in this section: freezing, water-bath canning, and pressure-cooking.

• FREEZE! •

Freezing food is a relatively easy process. Most fruits and vegetables, from artichokes to onions to zucchini, can be frozen, and many animal products can as well. (For step-by-step directions on how to freeze specific foods, visit the National Center for Home Food Preservation website, www.uga.edu/nchfp.)

Before beginning any food preservation process, you'll need to select fruits and vegetables to use. Ideally, you'll be getting much of the harvest from your own garden. If not, Riggs suggests shopping a local farmers' market or fruit stand, although those are sometimes more expensive. To save money, consider a trip to a "pick-your-own" farm, or you may get lucky finding high-quality product at a nearby grocery store.

"The rule of thumb is that the quality that you put in is what is going to come out," Riggs says. "You want the best quality food going in."

Choose produce that is at the peak of ripeness, firm to the touch, and free of bruising. Food preservation methods are not a good way to rescue off-prime produce.

• It's a Wrap •

Next, you'll want to have the right containers on hand. According to the National Center for Home Food Preservation, foods for the freezer must have proper packaging materials to protect their flavor, color, moisture content, and nutritive value from the dry climate of the freezer. Rigid plastic or glass containers, or flexible bags or wrappings work well. Liquid packs work especially well in plastic or glass containers because the straight sides make frozen food easier to get out. They are often reusable and more "green," plus they are easier to stack. However, glass jars can break at freezing temperatures.

Flexible bags or wrappings, such as butcher paper and plastic freezer bags, are ideal for dry-packed products with little or no liquid. They also work nicely for foods with irregular shapes. Whether you use the twist-tie or ziplock bags, you'll want to press the bag to remove as much air as possible before closing. A neat trick Natalie learned is to seal the bag almost entirely, leaving just enough room to insert a straw. Suck the excess air out of the straw and seal quickly.

• Packing It On •

Generally, fruits can be frozen using three methods: dry pack, syrup pack, or sugar pack. A dry pack is just as the name implies—fruit frozen as it is, without added liquid or sugar. This method works best for small whole fruits, like raspberries or blueberries. To dry pack, the simplest approach is to sort the fruit to remove leaves, stems, and defective berries. Wash, then pack the fruit into a container, seal, and freeze.

Another method, tray pack, may make fruit easier to remove from a container after frozen. To tray pack, prepare and wash fruit as usual. Then spread a single layer of fruit on shallow tray and freeze. After frozen, package and return to the freezer. This approach works best if you'd like to be able to open the container, use some of the fruit and then reseal the container. Natalie buys berries on sale and freezes them on large cookie sheets. Then she puts them into freezer bags and uses them in smoothies.

Fruits are also tasty when frozen in syrup or sugar. A syrup pack uses a combination of water and sugar to create a cold syrup that covers fruit in containers. The exact amount of sugar used depends on whether you want a very light, light, medium, heavy, or very heavy syrup. A very light syrup uses a half cup of sugar and four cups of water; a very heavy syrup uses four cups of sugar and four cups of water.

For a sugar pack, carefully mix sugar with berries and stir until most of the sugar is dissolved. Pack in containers, seal, and freeze.

No matter the method used, always leave at least a half an inch of headspace in containers for expansion, Riggs says. Otherwise, bags or containers can break or leak.

"When it comes to freezing, about anybody can do it," Riggs says. "You don't need special equipment; you just need a few basic tools and supplies. It's hard to mess it up."

• BLANCHING IS BEST •

The best way to freeze vegetables is to blanch them. Blanching is scalding vegetables in boiling water or steam for a short time, usually less than five minutes. The hot water halts enzyme actions that can eventually cause a loss of flavor, color, and texture. Blanching also helps clean the vegetables, preserves the color, and slows vitamin loss. By wilting or softening vegetables, it makes them easier to pack too.

All that's required is a cooking pot of boiling water, a sink of ice water, and citric acid or lemon juice, said Riggs.

To blanch, use one gallon of water per pound of prepared vegetables. Fit a wire basket into a large pot with a lid. Fill the basket with vegetables, lower into rapidly boiling water, and cover with a lid. According to the National Center for

Home Food Preservation, the water should return to boiling within one minute. If it doesn't, you have too many vegetables for the amount of water. Start timing blanching as soon as the water returns to a boil. Maintain boil for the duration of the time required for the vegetable you're working with.

As soon as blanching is finished, cool vegetables quickly to stop the cooking process. To cool, Riggs suggests plunging the basket of vegetables into ice-cold water. Make sure all the vegetables are immersed and then drain thoroughly.

Properly frozen produce can last between eight and twelve months at 0°F. For the best quality, freeze foods immediately after they are packed and sealed. Don't overload a freezer with unfrozen food. Leave space around new, warm packages to allow cold air to circulate freely around them. After they have frozen, stack and store the packages together so you'll be able to find them easily. Riggs advises following the "first in, first out" rule to rotate foods so that older items are used first.

• CAN IT •

Unlike freezing food, where a variety of approaches work well, using a pressure cooker or water bath canner to preserve food requires an exact approach.

"Canning is more of a science that requires special equipment and tools and knowledge of things like altitude," Riggs says.

Pressure canning is the safest method for preserving low-acid foods like salsa, red meats, seafood, poultry, and fresh vegetables. These low-acid foods require a higher temperature when processing than can be reached by placing them in a boiling water bath. Fruits, pickles, sauerkraut, jams, jellies, marmalades, and fruit butters or spreads fit the high-acid group and are appropriate for boiling water canning, also known as water-bath canning.

If you've never canned before, Riggs recommends mastering the water-bath method before you advance to pressure canning.

"One of the biggest excuses people give for canning is that they don't feel like they have the knowledge base to do it on their own," Riggs says. "If they call us, we try to match them up with somebody that already does it so they can get over the fear. It's really not complicated; you just have to follow instructions."

The first time Natalie used a boiling-water canner, she enlisted the help of a friend who had canned fruit and vegetables many times before. After canning a bushel of peaches—with nary a shattered jar in sight and all lids sealed—Natalie had enough confidence to continue on her own. Similarly, Elyssa first asked a friend to teach her how to make strawberry jam using a boiling-water canner before attempting it on her own.

If you want to barely get your feet wet, so to speak, with food preservation, start with jams and jellies, Riggs suggests. "Those are probably the easiest to do," she says. "You put the ingredients into a pot and cook it, then put it into jars and process it." The ingredients are minimal too: mainly fruit, sugar, and some pectin. "It is pretty straightforward, and if you mess it up, you can still use it for syrup." After mastering jams, move on to pears, cherries, peaches, and so forth.

❧ ESSENTIAL SUPPLIES

To get started with boiling-water canning, you'll need:

* water-bath canner or large pot (deep enough so that at least one inch of briskly boiling water will be over the tops of the jars during processing)
* canning rack for submersing jars
* jar lifter
* lid lifter
* funnel
* jars, lids, and bands (everything but the lids can be reused for years)
* thermometer

Up-front, canning may not be as cheap as purchasing commercially processed fruits and vegetables in the grocery store. But once you accumulate a supply of canning jars and the necessary equipment, the only annual costs should be new lids and produce if you don't grow it yourself. "After the first year or two, it is less expensive," Riggs said. Plus, it's hard to put a cost on the sense of accomplishment and perhaps peace of mind that comes from preserving your own food.

Boiling water canners and basic canning kits are available at many grocery stores and most superstores nationwide, like Walmart or Target.

WATER BATH BASICS

The basic process for using a boiling water canner is as follows:

1. Fill the canner halfway with water.

2. Preheat water to 140°F for raw-packed foods and to 180°F for hot-packed foods. (Raw- or cold-packed foods are those placed directly into hot jars and covered with hot syrup; hot-packed foods are partially cooked or heated through and placed hot into hot jars and covered with hot syrup.)

3. Load filled jars, fitted with lids, into the canner rack and use the handles to lower the rack into the water; or fill the canner, one jar at a time, with a jar lifter.

4. Add more boiling water, if needed, so the water level is at least 1 inch above jar tops.

5. Cover with the canner lid and turn heat up until water boils rapidly.

6. Set a timer for the required processing time.

7. Lower the heat setting to maintain a gentle but steady boil through processing.

8. Add more boiling water, as needed, to keep the water level one inch above jar lids.

9. When jars have been boiled for the recommended time, turn off the heat and remove the canner lid.

10. Using a jar lifter, remove the jars and place them on a protected surface, leaving at least one-inch spaces between the jars. Keep away from air drafts and let the jars cool at room temperature.

11. Do not touch until completely cooled. This may take from 12 to 24 hours.

12. When completely cooled, remove ring bands from sealed jars. Ring bands can be washed and reused next time. Put any unsealed jars in the refrigerator and use first.

13. Wash jars and lids to remove stickiness or other residue.

14. Label jars and store in a cool, dry place out of direct light.

15. To check the seal, press on the top of the lid after completely cooled. It should not move or make a sound. It you are able to press down or hear a clicking sound, the processing was not successful. You can discard the lid and reprocess with a new lid. Or keep that jar in the refrigerator and use immediately.

• UNDER PRESSURE •

As previously stated, pressure canning is a safe method for preserving low-acid foods that require a higher temperature to kill bacteria. The only way to reach that temperature of 240°F is by creating steam under pressure.

For pressure canning, you'll need:

❧ pressure canner with all parts accounted for and in good condition

❧ jar lifter

❧ canning jars, lids, and rings

Most modern pressure canners have a perforated metal rack or basket with handles, rubber gasket, a dial or weighted gauge, an automatic vent/cover lock, a steam vent (or vent port) that is closed with a counterweight or weighted gauge and a safety fuse. Riggs says there are two variations of pressure canners: ones with a dial gauge with numbers attached and others with a weighted gauge. With the latter, the rocking of the weight signals the end of the pressurization and is for "people that don't like to be tied to their canners." However, the former may be more precise in temperature, thus making it more difficult to undercook the food.

If you're buying a pressure canner, Riggs recommends selecting a national brand because replacement parts will be easier to find. Hand-me-down canners, from as early as the 1940s, may still be safe if they have been well cared for. However, if you're using a secondhand canner, make sure it has all of its parts.

"The best idea is to make sure you've had your canner tested for accuracy," Riggs said. "That is a service that is done at extension centers."

PRESSURE CANNING STEPS

The basic process for using a pressure canner is as follows:

1. Center the canner over the burner. When you have your jars of food ready for canning, put the rack and hot water into the canner. If the amount of water is not specified with a given food, use 2 to 3 inches of water. Longer processes require more water. Some specific products require that you start with even more water in the canner. Always follow the directions with USDA processes for specific foods. For hot-packed foods, bring the water to 180°F ahead of time but be careful not to boil the water or heat it long enough for depth to decrease. For raw-packed foods, the water should only be brought to 140°F.

2. Place filled jars, fitted with lids, on the jar rack in the canner, using a jar lifter. When moving jars with a jar lifter, make sure the jar lifter is securely positioned below the neck of the jar (below the screw band of the lid). Keep the jar upright at all times. Tilting the jar could cause food to spill into the sealing area of the lid.

3. Fasten the canner lid securely. Leave the weight off the vent port or open the petcock.

4. Turn the heat setting to its highest position. Heat until the water boils and steam flows freely in a funnel shape from the open vent port or petcock. While maintaining the high heat setting, let the steam flow continuously for 10 minutes.

5. After this venting of the canner, place the counterweight or weighted gauge on the vent port or close the petcock. The canner will pressurize during the next three to ten minutes.

6. Start timing the process when the pressure reading on the dial gauge indicates that the recommended pressure has been reached, or, for canners without dial gauges, when the weighted gauge begins to jiggle or rock as the manufacturer describes.

7. Regulate the heat under the canner to maintain a steady pressure at, or slightly above, the correct gauge pressure. Loss of pressure at any time can result in under-processing or unsafe food. If at any time pressure goes below the recommended amount, bring the canner back to pressure and start the timing of the process from the beginning.

8. When the timed process is completed, turn off the heat, remove the canner from the heat if possible and let the canner cool down naturally. While it is cooling, it is also depressurizing. Do not force cool the canner with methods like cold running water or opening the vent port before fully depressurized. Forced cooling may result in food spoilage.

9. After the canner is completely depressurized, remove the weight from the vent port or open the petcock. Wait ten minutes, then unfasten the lid and remove it carefully. Lift the lid with the underside away from you so that the steam coming out of the canner does not burn you.

10. Using a jar lifter, remove the jars one at a time, being careful not to tilt the jars. Carefully place them directly onto a towel or a cooling rack, leaving at least one inch of space between the jars during

cooling. Avoid placing the jars on a cold surface or in a cold draft.

11. Let the jars sit undisturbed while they cool, from twelve to twenty-four hours. Do not tighten ring bands on the lids or push down on the center of the flat metal lid until the jar is completely cooled.

12. Remove ring bands from sealed jars. Ring bands can be washed and dried and put away for using another time. Put any unsealed jars in the refrigerator and use first.

13. Wash jars and lids to remove all residues.

14. Label jars and store in a cool, dry place out of direct light.

• DO'S AND DON'TS •

Canning is a straightforward science—not an outlet for creative expression. People get into trouble when they start making up their own recipes, Riggs says, and this is especially worrisome with high-acid foods like salsas. "Adding extra onions, chilies, bell peppers, and other vegetables to salsas isn't a good idea," Riggs says. "Extra vegetables dilute the acidity and can result in botulism poisoning." Instead, use USDA-approved recipes that have been scientifically tested.

Other major do's and don'ts include

- **Do** adjust for altitude. Boiling temperatures are lower at higher altitudes, so products will be under-processed unless adjustments are made. Pressure canning requires adding more pounds of pressure, while boiling water canning requires more processing time.

- **Don't** add extra starch, flour, or other thickeners to recipes. This will slow the rate of heat penetration and can result in undercooking. If you like thicker salsas, for instance, use a verified recipe for canning and add thickening agent rights before you are going to use it.

- **Do** vent a pressure canner. Insufficient venting can result in cold spots that will not reach the high temperature needed for safe canning.

- ❧ **Don't** cool pressure canner under running water. Hurrying the cool-down process can result in under-processed food. Also, jars could break.

- ❧ **Do** process hot-packed food right away. Letting hot-packed foods cool before processing could lead to under-processing. Canned meat, vegetables, or salsa that is under-processed can cause botulism. Fruits that aren't adequately processed may spoil quickly or grow mold.

- ❧ **Don't** get too experimental. Riggs says she occasionally gets calls from people who are trying to can quick breads, hydrated wheat berries, or butter. Right now, there isn't any research that supports canning these items in-home. "We encourage people to follow tested guidelines and use up-to-date, scientifically tested recipes," Riggs says. If you want to make your own salsa, she suggests you freeze it instead.

For the highest quality, use home-canned goods within two to three years of canning. Rotate your supply, using the oldest products before newer ones. "Don't can more than you're going to use within a few years," Riggs says.

To keep from getting burned out, she also suggests canning several years of one product at once. For instance, put away three years of corn one summer. The year after that, can fruits. The third year, preserve fruits. Heed her advice: "Don't get burned out doing a little of everything all year long."

BEYOND WISHY-WASHY
Clothing Care and Repair

Laundry may be a chore, but it doesn't have to feel like one. For years, Natalie dreaded doing the laundry. She fretted over sorting clothes, unsure if she was combining the right colors. She felt perplexed by detergent choices in the laundry aisle at the store and was utterly depressed by the amount of time she spent removing stains from clothing.

Then she found Mary Marlowe Leverette's About.com Guide to Laundry.[1] Leverette is a former Clemson University Extension Agent and laundry expert who has shared her knowledge in publications like *Real Simple* magazine, *Women's Health* magazine, Proctor and Gamble's *Everyday Solutions* newsletter, and on Martha Stewart Living Radio. She's had more than forty years of experience in the real world of laundry, growing up on a farm and raising two sons.

It's safe to say Leverette has got laundry down to a science. And she says it's a task you should master too.

"How you handle laundry is actually a financial investment," she says. "Proper laundering preserves your clothing and lessens how often you must replace the garments. It is also a financial investment in yourself to present your best appearance."

Having the right attitude about laundry should help lighten its psychological load, so to speak. Instead of merely doing laundry, you're saving money, preserving your wardrobe, and improving your image!

• COMING CLEAN •

Everything comes out in the wash. Or so the idiom goes. But if you're not doing laundry correctly, you may find that next to nothing comes out in the wash. And that is where discouragement—and stains—can set in.

Leverette breaks laundry into twelve basic steps:

1. *Check the labels.* The tag should say if an item is machine washable. If it's not, put it in a bag to go to the dry cleaner's. If the label says "wash separately" or "hand-wash," sort those into a separate pile.

2. *Sort by color.* Whites and other light colors, such as pastels or prints with white backgrounds are one pile. Dark colors, like navy, brown or black are another pile.

3. *Sort again by fabric type.* Towels and sheets go in their own pile. Heavier-weighted apparel, like denim jeans or sweatshirts, should be separated from T-shirts and blouses. This will make it easier to choose the appropriate washing and drying temperatures. (Generally heavier items can withstand a lot more abuse).

4. *Assess piles.* If there aren't enough, say, jeans to make a full load, recombine them with other items within the color range (light or dark) and wash together. Cater the cycle to the most delicate items included.

5. *Select your detergent,* reading directions for proper use. Most directions advise adding detergent before loading clothes to prevent soap buildup on clothing.

6. *Select temperature settings.* Generally, most clothes can be washed in cold water, unless they are caked with dirt. This should help keep your bill down and can prevent laundry disasters caused by hot water, such as bleeding colors. Leverette recommends always rinsing with cold water.

7. *Check pockets* for tissue, papers, cell phones, and other random items. Remove accessories, like belts or jewelry, from apparel. Close zippers and buttons.

8. *Load clothing into machine one item at a time.* Don't wad up and shove in. Knitted items, corduroy, textured fabric and sweatshirts may be turned inside out to protect fabric finishes.

9. *If laundering bed sheets and towels,* wash at the highest recommended temperature at least every other wash to sanitize.

10. *After washing cycle is complete,* immediately move wet laundry out of machine. Hang air-dry items and place other items in dryer.

11. *If you didn't separate loads by fabric type for washing,* do it now. Dry similar weight items together to prevent shrinking and protect clothing.

12. *To prevent wrinkling,* fold or hang each piece of clothing immediately.

To follow these steps, you'll need access to a washing machine, laundry detergent, and an automatic dryer or clothesline. If you don't have access to a washing machine, good luck! Just kidding. Look for tips on hand-washing clothes further in the chapter.

• CYCLING THROUGH MISTAKES •

Leverette's steps are straightforward and likely familiar to most. But there is more to laundry than just going through the motions. For starters, Leverette says that most people pile on laundry detergent when it simply isn't necessary.

"With today's highly programmed washers, most people can end up with a clean load of wet clothes. However, almost everyone uses too much detergent," she says. "This is expensive and leaves residue on our laundry that keeps it from being its brightest or whitest."

Overdrying clothes, not sorting by color, and forgetting to treat stains are other mistakes she cites. Although it's not on Leverette's list, Natalie swears she's not the only one who has filled a machine with water and detergent but forgotten to put clothes in. Or done a late-night load of laundry and failed to move the clothes to the dryer. If you haven't experienced it for yourself, trust us—there are few smells worse than sour laundry.

• WHAT ELSE CAN GO AWRY •

- **WHITES** aren't bright: Gray or yellow whites could be a sign you're using water that isn't quite warm enough for the fabric. Or maybe you're overloading your washer. Soil from really dirty clothes can resettle on mildly dirty clothes and make them dull.

- **COLORS FADE**: Turn dark-colored clothes inside-out to avoid too much wear and tear.

- **CLOTHING SHRINKS**: The best way to avoid "mini-me" clothing is to use cold water washes and hang clothing to dry.

- **COLOR BLEEDS**: Don't wash whites with darks. Dyes could run and ruin lighter-colored clothing. To find out if an item is colorfast, put a drop of water on an inside corner or seam and see if the dye runs. If it does, hand-wash separately.

- **DELICATES LOOK LESS DAINTY**: Hand-wash unmentionables in a sink filled with cool water. When machine washing bras, place in a mesh lingerie bag and use the delicate cycle.

- **STAINS REMAIN**: Don't ever put a stained garment in the dryer unless you want the stain to stay there forever. Act on stains as soon as possible. If they don't come out in the wash, try again. Use bleach as a last-ditch effort.

- **CLOTHES ARE WRINKLED**: Use dryer sheets or fabric softener to reduce wrinkles. Use the lowest temperature setting that will still dry clothing.

• DETERGENT DILEMMAS •

There are so many laundry products on the market today that most grocery stores and super stores have dedicated an entire aisle to them. If you've ever gone to pick up detergent only to end up hemming and hawing over which one to buy, you're not alone.

Nearly every time Natalie needs to restock on laundry essentials, she ends up standing in the aisle for a good ten minutes, doing per-load cost comparisons and inspecting ingredients while her children chatter (or sometimes scream) in the background. She never really makes any headway differentiating between products and typically ends up grabbing whatever it is she's always used. Elyssa has super-sensitive skin and is always looking for a gentle detergent that won't irritate it.

Leverette says selecting soap needn't be so hard. Unlike a good man, a good detergent is not hard to find. It's all a matter of what works best for you. Generally, powdered detergents work well for general loads and are usually less expensive. Liquid detergents, which usually contain enzymes, are good for pretreating stains and removing food.

"Over the years, I have tried many, many different detergents and found the formula that works well for the average level of soil on my family's clothes," Leverette says. "If something is particularly soiled, I add baking soda to boost detergent performance. For really tough soil, I will use an oxygen or chlorine-based bleach as appropriate. Use coupons and store sales to try different brands. This is particularly important if someone in your family has sensitive skin or allergies. Your personal choice should be one that works well for you."

• BREAKING DOWN DETERGENTS •

Both liquid and powdered detergents can be used in cold water. However, Leverette cautions that some powdered detergents don't dissolve well in lower temperatures. (Hence the "cold water" detergents on the market). If you have this problem, use a higher wash temperature or dissolve the powder in a cup of hot water before adding it to the wash.

- Most brands of liquid and powdered detergent are available in concentrated or ultra-concentrated forms. Make sure you read the label and use the right amount.

- When examining choices, you may notice combination detergents. Like, say, a detergent plus fabric softener or color-safe bleach or bleach alternative. Leverette says some of these features enhance a detergent's performance, but you'll likely need to test it to see how.

↭ If you own a lot of delicate items, you may already be familiar with specialty detergents, designed for hand-washing or machine-washing less-than-robust apparel and unmentionables. There are also fragrance and dye-free detergents made for baby's laundry or for people with allergies or sensitive skin.

↭ The buy-what-works-for-you wisdom can be extended to the plethora of stain removers, pretreatments, boosters, and the like that pepper laundry aisles.

↭ No matter what kind you use, try using one-half less than the recommended amount. It's likely your clothes will come out just as clean and you'll save money.

• PANTRY FIXES •

Stocking up on laundry supplies can be a hit to the budget, more so if you routinely use detergent and stain removers in the wash, and fabric softener and fabric sheets or bars in the dryer. However, Leverette has hints on how to save some pennies.

"I have a small family, and I use commercial detergent for convenience; and by using less than the recommended amount, I find it to be quite economical," she says. "I do use white vinegar and baking soda regularly in the laundry to boost performance and keep my washer running well."

Inexpensive white vinegar (found readily in bulk at warehouse stores like Sam's Club or Costco) can be used to whiten, brighten, reduce odor, and remove mildew. It is also a green alternative to other chemical products. Leverette advises keeping a spray bottle filled with distilled white vinegar on hand in the laundry room. To remove sweat odor and stains on clothing, spray vinegar on underarm and collar areas as you're tossing items into the wash. Vinegar will cut through residual deodorant left on clothing and prevent underarm yellowing.

Baking soda is another green fix Leverette regularly uses to boost detergent and bleach performance, soften clothes, and control suds. A large box of baking soda will only set you back a few dollars; look for boxes labeled "for household use" to get the best bang for your buck.

According to Leverette, "Odors in our laundry are caused by bacteria. They can usually be removed as the detergent molecules break up the bacteria cells. In certain types of water and with some bacteria, the detergent needs a boost to work more effectively.

Baking soda helps to regulate the pH level in the washer water by keeping it from being too acidic or too alkaline. By adding a half cup of baking soda to each laundry load, detergents can work more effectively and reduce bacteria."

Because it is a natural mineral, baking soda is less harsh than the synthetic perfumes used in some detergents to mask odors.

• DIY DETERGENT •

If you are highly concerned about chemicals hiding in commercial laundry detergents or really want to save cash, consider making your own laundry detergent. Leverette posted a recipe online that uses only four ingredients and takes approximately fifteen minutes to make. Depending on your previous detergent, you can save about thirty cents per load of laundry, she says.

Here are her steps:

1. Using a regular cheese grater, grate a bar of pure soap—Ivory, Kirk's

Castile, or Fels Naptha soaps. One 5.5-ounce bar will make about one cup of flakes.

2. In a large, resealable container, combine 1 cup soap flakes, 1 cup baking soda, 1 cup washing soda (sodium carbonate), and ½ cup borax. Washing soda is caustic to the skin, so you should wear rubber gloves.

3. Mix ingredients well. Keep dry. Use ½ cup of mixture per load of laundry.

• OUT, DARN SPOT •

Nothing can ruin a perfectly good article of clothing like a stubborn stain. Desperately trying to remove a spot with little results can be maddening. At times, it has us paraphrasing Shakespeare.

Keep in mind: not every stain can be removed, Leverette says. "I've met a few that will never come out, and those garments become my gardening or painting clothes. But there are really only a few basic types of stains—protein based, oil based, dye based, and combination. Once you master those techniques for removal, you're ready for most everything."

Follow these directions for stain removal on machine-washable fabrics. Head to Leverette's laundry.about.com page for more detailed troubleshooting.

PROTEIN STAINS: Include baby food, formula, blood, egg, milk, or ice cream. Soak with cold water before washing. Never use hot water. It can actually cook the stain and imbed it deeper into the fabric fibers. For old or dried protein stains, scrape off what you can and soak in cold water using a liquid detergent with color-safe bleach. After presoaking for thirty minutes, wash in warm water with detergent. Soak again if stain remains and rewash.

OIL STAINS: Include butter, salad dressing, hand lotion, and automotive oil. Use a solvent-based pretreatment, like Shout or Spray 'n Wash. Follow directions as indicated on pretreatment bottle, then

151.

wash in hottest water possible for the type of fabric. Check to make sure the stain has been removed before drying. Repeat if necessary.

෪ **TANNIN STAINS**: Include juice and soft drinks, ketchup, salsa, and berries. Natural soaps will set the stain, so avoid those. Remove these types of stains by laundering the garment using detergent in the hottest water recommended for the fabric.

෪ **DYE STAINS**: Include grass, red foods, and felt-tip pens. These are hard to remove. You'll need to pretreat (see instructions under oil stains), then soak and, if necessary, use color-safe bleach to remove the stain.

෪ **COMBINATION STAINS**: Includes ballpoint ink, crayon, gravy, and makeup. These stains contain both an oil or wax component and a dye or pigment component. Follow the directions for oil stains first, and then tackle the dye stain. If you take your time, most will come out completely.

෪ **MYSTERY STAINS**: Use gentlest stain removal method first. Soak it in cold water for a minimum of thirty minutes. Then use liquid detergent and warm water to wash. Rinse and air dry. If stain persists, wash with an all-fabric oxygen bleach in warm water. Air dry again. As a last resort on colorfast or white clothing, try a diluted solution of chlorine bleach.

• SPONGE ON, SPONGE OFF •

Spot treatments are often part of the stain removal process. This is sometimes called "sponging," Leverette says, and is useful for confining the stain to a small area and keeping it from spreading.

Start with a flat surface covered with a clean white cloth or paper towels to absorb the stain. Place the garment's stained area face down over the padding. Dampen a small white cloth with the recommended cleaning solvent. Use the cloth to pat the stain from the wrong side. Feather the edges of the stain, working from the outside in to keep the stain from enlarging. As the stain transfers from the garment to the white padding, move the garment to a clean place on the padding so the stain continues to transfer. Repeat until gone, then wash as directed.

• HANDY TO KNOW •

Ignoring hand-wash and dry-clean-only labels is risky business.

"Unless you are an experienced launderer, believe the labels," Leverette says. "Following the directions will protect your garment and give it the best possible results. While the outer fabric may be something machine-washable—like cotton—the interior structure of the garment may not withstand the rigors of the wash cycle."

If you no longer want to spend money or take the effort to have an article of clothing specially cleaned, go ahead and try including it in the wash, she says. But be prepared to replace the garment.

Another way to save money may be to try home dry cleaning kits. They don't clean better than a professional cleaner—you miss out on that crisply pressed look—but they are convenient and less expensive per garment cleaned, Leverette says.

Hand-washing is a good idea for delicate fabrics, like silk or lace, vintage clothing, lingerie and other items you want to take extra care with. To hand-wash, pretreat stains according to type. Dissolve the specified amount of a delicate detergent, such as Woolite, in a plugged sink filled with cold water. Let the items soak for at least fifteen minutes. Rinse, then wring by hand or roll in a towel to remove moisture. Hang or lay flat to dry.

• TOOLS OF THE TRADE •

The most useful tools for laundering clothing are also the most expensive: a washing machine and an automatic dryer. While most people would likely agree that the former is essential, an automatic dryer can be replaced with an indoor or outdoor clothesline if you have the space, Leverette says.

Even if you do have a dryer, a clothesline is helpful for hand-wash-only items or clothes that may shrink or become misshapen in the dryer. An alternative is a drying rack, which can be freestanding or wall-mounted. A sink in the laundry room or nearby is helpful for soaking stained items or hand-washing clothes. It's also helpful to have an ironing board and iron, a sectioned hamper, and a shelf to hold detergents and stain removers.

"I find white cleaning cloths for blotting away stains and a soft scrub brush are used almost every laundry day," Leverette adds.

• WHEN AND WHY •

Now you know how to do the laundry. But when should you do it?

According to Leverette, Monday was the traditional wash day for hundreds of years. With that task accomplished, a homemaker could iron on Tuesday and clear the rest of the week for weekend meal preparation and the Sabbath.

Modern conveniences mean laundry takes way less time than it used to. You won't likely need to labor over laundry for twelve hours straight. Leverette suggests discovering your own system, whether that be once a day or once a week.

"I think every person or family needs to find what works best for them. I have a small family—two sons—and I do laundry once per week. By then, we have accumulated enough white, colored, delicates, sheets, and towels to do a full load (I hate wasting water). As my mother aged, she did very small loads almost every day because it fit her energy level and gave her a sense of accomplishment."

154

Like Leverette, we like to do our laundry on a schedule, but it usually takes two days to clean all of our families' clothing. Still, there is nothing like the feeling of putting away the last folded garment and having only empty hampers—even if the hampers are only empty for a few hours. In fact, on the rare occasion Elyssa can get every item of clothing laundered before her husband and boys come home with a new pile of muddy laundry, she does a victory lap around her house, punching the air and singing the theme from the movie *Rocky*—it's that big of an accomplishment.

Once you've found your laundry groove, stay on top of the task, Leverette advises, because catching up can be hard to do.

"Teach everyone in the family to do laundry and enlist their help. You'll be amazed at how much even a young child can help," she says.

• SEW EASY •

If you're in charge of clothing care, you're likely heading up clothing repair too. And that's where basic sewing and mending skills come in handy. (Advanced skills don't hurt either.)

When Natalie was in high school, her mom, Shelley, went to a local department store and bought four sewing machines: one for each of her four daughters. Shelley had learned to sew in high school and had been using the essential skill ever since. She made her daughters and son matching pajamas at Christmastime and whipped up costumes for Halloween. She wanted to teach the handy homemaking skill to her daughters, in keeping with Latter-day Saint principles of provident living and self-reliance. Now, most of the girls are holding onto the tradition—even if some of their skills may be hanging by a thread.

Elyssa laughed when her mom bought her a sewing machine in college. Her mind filled with images of old-fashioned bonnets and funny-looking jeans. Several years and sewing classes later, Elyssa has realized her sewing machine is one of her most useful tools.

Sewing and mending may seem to some like antiquated tasks. Rather than take the time to repair minor rips, patch holes or secure buttons, many people either have their damaged clothing sent to the tailor or thrown out with the trash. Either choice is far more expensive than repairing clothing yourself—and you don't have to be Suzy Homemaker to give it a go.

"I think that the tides are turning now and sewing is coming back into vogue," said Carrie Lundell, a children's fashion designer and mother of four in Orange County, California. "People always say to me, 'I wish I would've learned this when I was younger.'"[2]

Lundell's mother was big on sewing and vowed that none of her daughters would leave the house without becoming competent. She took time to teach them one-on-one, and even though some of the girls disliked sewing at the time, they are now grateful their mother showed them how. For Lundell, the basic skills learned at her mother's side were a starting point for her career. At Brigham Young University, she majored in fashion design. Immediately after graduation, she worked for a children's clothing company in Los Angeles, and then she worked for retailer Old Navy in New York City. After the birth of her first baby, she began freelance designing from home. Now she blogs about sewing and other adventures at ThisMamaMakesStuff.com

Although Lundell has taken her needle-and-thread skills to the next level, she is the first to attest that you don't have to be a professional to sew.

"It is easy to learn how to sew," she says, "and it can really save you a lot of money. With practice, it is easy and fun and not a chore."

• MONEY-SAVING STITCHES •

A major reason many people give for not learning how to sew is the cost. They think it is too expensive to make homemade gifts, clothing, or décor—and depending on the circumstances, those people may be right. In fact, the first time Elyssa made a quilt, she foolishly spent almost a hundred dollars on fabric. She figured the quilt cost about four times as much as a cheaply made blanket from a retail store. But it's one of Elyssa's most prized possessions, all the more loved because of its wobbly and uneven stitching.

Lundell said, "You can spend a lot of money on fabric and trims and buttons and zippers and patterns. People can make clothes so cheaply in other countries that you're not really saving money sewing clothes from scratch. But sewing saves you money when it comes to mending and repairs and alterations."

For instance, when her husband loses weight, she takes his pants in. When he gains the weight back, she can let them out. Hemming jeans or skirts is never cause for a pricey visit to a tailor.

"Some of the most useful skills I've learned are hemming, taking in waists, tapering pants, and putting sleeves on dresses," Lundell says.

When one of her two daughters or her son puts a hole into a pair of pants or accidentally snags a shirt, she can fix it up quickly and put the garment back into service.

Natalie's son wears holes into jeans like they're going out of style. Every time a new rip emerges, she pulls out her sewing machine and puts her high school sewing class skills to work. Patching up the holes makes the jeans last for a few more months—until he rips another hole so wide that there is no sense in fixing them. But instead of tossing the worn-out jeans in the garbage, she keeps them for reuse in future jean repairs or other projects.

• MACHINE MADE •

You don't need a lot of gear to get started in sewing. For minor repairs, a variety of needles, matching thread, and scissors for cutting the strings are all that is needed. If you're worried about poking your thumb, buy a thimble.

At the next level, patches may be required, but these are readily available at fabric stores (and can even be found at larger grocery stores).

If you're ready to purchase a machine, Lundell suggests buying at a reputable sewing machine shop in your area.

"Go to a sewing machine shop, sit down, and sew on the machine," she says. "Usually the sewing machines that are the cheapest will actually cause you the most headache. You'll just want to scream because they're so frustrating. Cheaper machines have constant hiccups and you'll be constantly rethreading them."

You want to spend your time sewing, not reading through a hefty manual trying to figure out why your needle won't budge an inch. Although paying more up front may be a bit harder on your wallet, it'll be worth it once you stick with sewing. Many people who start on a cheaper machine give up sewing entirely because even minor projects take too much time.

Now, Lundell isn't suggesting that you spend your inheritance on a designer embroidery machine with all the bells and whistles. Rather, instead of spending a hundred dollars on a cheap machine on eBay.com, buy a three-hundred-dollar sewing machine from a local shop.

"I like machines with heavier parts," she said. "Some of the cheaper machines feel really light and are often made of plastic parts that break pretty easily."

When purchasing her most recent sewing machine, at the suggestion of a shop worker, Lundell pulled a line of thread through several different sewing machines so she could see the difference in ease. If you have a hard time pulling thread through the machine without breaking it, chances are the machine is going to have a rough time too.

The staff at a specialty sewing store should be able to fit you with the best machine for your purposes. Another perk: lessons are usually free with the purchase of a new machine. At the very least, you'll be taught how to thread the machine, wind a bobbin, and switch stitches.

• Back to School •

Once you've purchased a machine, take some time to familiarize yourself with the parts. Consider enrolling in a basic sewing class if lessons weren't included with your purchase. These are often available at community centers as well as fabric and sewing stores. A class should give you a rudimentary understanding of how your machine works, how to use it (sew!), and how to keep it running well. Even if you already know how to sew a straight line, the classes may be helpful from a maintenance standpoint.

• On Pins . . . •

One Christmas when she was a teenager, Natalie's paternal grandmother gave her a fold-and-go sewing kit the size of a birdhouse. The contents included a dozen or so small spools of thread, several kinds of needles, collapsible scissors, and a seam ripper. More years later than she'd like to admit, Natalie still has and

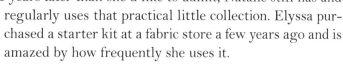

regularly uses that practical little collection. Elyssa purchased a starter kit at a fabric store a few years ago and is amazed by how frequently she uses it.

On a basic level, Lundell recommends a seam ripper, a good-quality pair of scissors, a pincushion, measuring tape, pins, needles, and a tool for marking fabric, such as tailor's chalk or a disappearing ink marking pen. Lundell saves soap shards from their inevitable demise down the drain, dries them out, and uses those to mark fabric. Seriously.

The type of pins you use is entirely up to you. Dressmaker's pins typically have a flat head, and ball pins are topped with brightly colored plastic balls. Packages of pins usually include several hundred, so you won't need to replace them too often.

• . . . AND NEEDLES •

You'll need several kinds of needles to operate a sewing machine, and they'll need to be replaced often. According to Lundell, one of the biggest mistakes that people make when sewing is to use the same needle forever. "People don't change their needles enough," she says. "A dull needle can make your machine go all wacky, and it can also damage the fabric too." Replace the needles on your sewing machine every two to three projects or after hitting a pin or otherwise damaging the needle. If you're having problems with missed or uneven stitches, chances are high your needle needs to be replaced.

There are different sizes and types of needles, each suited to a distinct fabric. Each needle is assigned a number. The European metric sizing numbers needles 60 to 110; American needles are sized 8 to 18. (Most packages include both numbers, displayed 11/80, for example).

The lower the number, the finer the needle. The higher the number, the larger the needle. When selecting the needles you'll need for a project, keep in mind that the lighter the fabric, the smaller the needle size needed. And vice-versa. If you're using a fine thread, you'll also want to use a smaller needle.

There are several types of needles, including regular point, ball-point, denim, twin, hemstitch, and wing needles. If you have a fancy embroidery machine, you'll likely need to keep a wider selection of needles on hand. For the rest of us, regular and ball-point needles in a variety of sizes will do.

Regular-point needles are typically used when sewing any woven material. When sewing with knit fabrics, you must use a ball-point needle. "Knit fabric is created in a different way than woven fabric, so using a sharp (regular-point) needle on a knit fabric will cut your threads. That cut can start to run in the fabric," Lundell said. Like the name implies, a ball-point needle has a bulbous end that helps the needle navigate between the loops that create knit fabric. A sharper, regular-point needle will chop right through it.

Use your fabric as a guide to determine what size of needle you'll need. For instance, sheer or lightweight woven fabric calls for a regular-point needle size

4/70 or 11/80; knit fabric of the same weight uses 10/70 or 12/80. Medium-weight broadcloth, corduroy, or velvet uses a 14/90; denim or canvas calls for a denim needle. The packaging on needles will spell this out for you, so all you need to know to get it right is the weight and kind of fabric you are working with.

For convenience purposes, we recommend buying several kinds and sizes of needles to have on hand for future projects. You don't have to clear the shelves, just keep enough for spur-of-the-moment projects and repairs. And don't stock up on specialty needles, like wedge point or twin, unless you have a specific project in mind.

• THREAD-BARE •

Grabbing thread from a bin at the dollar store is tempting. But resist the urge to buy cheap thread, Lundell says. "You can pay up front for good sewing thread or pay after the fact in sewing machine repairs."

And she speaks from experience. Days before Halloween one year, Lundell was furiously working on a costume for one of her children when her sewing machine threw her for a loop. The tension was wacky, the noises clunky. Frantically, she called the shop where she purchased her machine, where she was told over the phone that it was likely her thread rebelling. Dubious, she took the machine down to the shop, where it was rethreaded with more expensive, good-quality thread and ran as smooth as butter.

Cheap thread looks fuzzy up close. It is made from lots of pieces of thread joined together, and each joint creates small bumps along the thread. And each bump creates, well, bumps in the road. Pricier thread is spun from longer threads and is less prone to breaking.

There are a handful of general-purpose threads. Cotton, silk, nylon, polyester, and cotton-wrapped polyester are probably the most common. Polyester thread is commonly called "all-purpose thread." Because of its give, it is suitable for use on woven and knit fabrics. Cotton thread has no give and works well only on woven fabrics. Silk thread is recommended for silk and wool fabrics. Nylon thread is best for light- to medium-weight synthetics.

• GO, GO GADGET •

Beyond the basics, what you decide to invest in up to you. Over time, Lundell has upgraded some of her tools and found a few gadgets that work well for her. She found a set of pinking shears at an estate sale, and she finally traded in the pincushion she'd been using since high school (made for her by an old boyfriend's mom) for a pin catcher she made herself. Instead of going the traditional route by pinning a pattern to fabric and cutting around with scissors, Lundell uses fabric weights and a rotary cutter on a self-healing mat. "Unless it is something tiny and intricately shaped, I find this approach so much easier," she said.

She also uses an expanding button gauge, a loop turner, and a bamboo pointer to poke out corners. But when she didn't have that, she used the ends of her scissors.

Since so few items are actually crucial to accomplishing your sewing projects, it may be wise to spend a little more money on those initial purchases. There really is a difference between using cheap scissors bought at a superstore and more expensive scissors from a fabric shop. "A nice pair of scissors is really great to have," Lundell admits. She uses Gingher scissors, in case you're wondering.

You once get rolling with projects, you'll likely need to gather buttons, elastic, ribbon, or zippers, but hold off on purchasing unless you find a screaming deal. You'll save more money picking up notions on an as-needed basis.

• FABRICATION •

When purchasing fabric for projects, it may be hard to think providently. Natalie has a hard time not buying at least a few new yards of material every time she goes to the fabric store. Even if she doesn't have an immediate use in mind, she reasons that it is good to have cute fabric on hand and that she'll end up saving money in the long run. Her husband may tell another story, though, and that's why she should be more like Lundell, who rarely purchases brand-new textiles. "I can't remember the last time I bought fabric at a fabric store," she said. "Unless it is something specific that I need—a certain color lining or particular color to finish a project—I never buy fabric at the fabric store. Cost-wise, it doesn't make sense to me."

So where does she get her fabric from? Thrift stores, estate sales, garage sales, and the like. "I'll buy sheets at the thrift store or find clothing that is really big that I can cut up and use as fabric," she says.

- ⚜ All fabric should be prewashed before using, anyway, so the fact that fabric is used (or "vintage," if you prefer to give it a more romantic title) really makes no difference. When buying fabric secondhand, you'll want to scour it for holes or stains that would make it less usable.

- ⚜ If you must buy fabric brand new, consider shopping at discount fabric shops or stores that put out coupons to lower your out-of-pocket expenses.

- ⚜ Before you head out to purchase fabric, new or used, shop your own stash! See if you have material that will work for your project.

• WHERE TO PUT IT ALL •

While many hobbyists like to hoard yards of fabric, with coordinating notions, waiting, you don't need it to be a proficient and efficient seamstress.

What is helpful, though, is some type of dedicated space for sewing. Lundell currently lives in a three-bedroom house. Previously, she lived in a small city apartment. She has never had a sewing room but instead relies on an inexpensive secretary cabinet that houses her machine. "It's a really small profile when it is all closed-up, and I only open it when it is time to sew," she said. Lundell keeps plastic bins with fabric and other supplies in her garage, bringing them into her house as needed.

Pick a spot with sufficient lighting, so you can see what you're doing. It is also nice to have flat surface nearby for cutting out fabric. Natalie often uses the kitchen table and sometimes puts her self-healing mat on the carpet so she can cut and watch TV. Elyssa has a "craft table" in her basement—also near a TV—that she uses for sewing and other projects. See chapter ten on organization for more details on arranging your space.

• IN STITCHES •

Now that you've gathered all the right tools, you're well on your way to a successful first project. Choose one that is straightforward. Don't make anything that calls for a zipper or buttons, or even has lots of steps. "I have a lot of people come to me saying, 'This is too hard. I'm not doing this again,' because they've picked a project that is over their head," Lundell says.

Before starting, prewash fabric and dry to prevent shrinkage after the fact. (Unless you're using home décor fabric that won't ever require washing). Read pattern directions carefully and make sure you understand the process. Careful attention will save you a lot of time unpicking stitches after the fact. Natalie's husband will attest to the time this takes, as she often recruits him to unpick stitches while watching ESPN. (She sews mostly at night after the kids are in bed, a move that always increases the mistake quotient).

Start projects with a straight fabric edge. This is especially important if you're using a pattern, which could otherwise end up tilted or crooked. You can find a straight edge by making a small cut at the cross grain then tearing by hand. The fabric will tear straight across, leaving you with an even edge.

As your skills develop, you may discover shortcuts and other time-savers when following patterns. Cut corners if you want to—not literally, of course—but try not to skip pressing fabric as directed. Using an iron to flatten hems and seams really makes a difference in the finished product.

At the end of the chapter are suggestions and directions for a few beginner sewing projects, including hemming pants, and patching a hole by hand.

• REFASHIONING •

Once you gain some confidence in basic sewing, it's time to take on refashions. Inexpensive and earth-friendly, a refashion is any project that repurposes outdated or not-functional clothing into an item that is a better fit for you (and your wardrobe).

Refashions are often spontaneous. You can follow a pattern if you'd like, or use your skills and creativity to create a one-of-a-kind garment.

Lundell started refashioning several years ago after realizing she was spending way too much money on clothes for her kids. Much of the clothing she bought was in the name of research—she is a children's clothing designer, after all—but after quitting her full-time job to stay home with her kids, she couldn't justify the expense. Going cold turkey by avoiding clothing stores completely seemed like the only solution. So she took a refashioning pledge online and went almost two years without buying any clothes for her kids, she says. "It made me realize that my kids always had way too many clothes," she says. "I also realized that I prefer making things for them over just going out and buying. Anytime I wanted to go out and look for something, I would just sit down and make something."

• CHEAP AND CHIC •

Lundell has dozens of examples and tutorials posted on her blog, ThisMamaMakesStuff.com, if you're looking for inspiration. She suggests starting with clothing you already own that is stained, ripped, or otherwise cast off. Then you can take a page from Lundell's book and transform two thrifted tablecloths and a secondhand crocheted poncho into two Christmas dresses and a tie. Or recycle an old screen-printed T-shirts into baby gowns. Or turn a dowdy dress into a trendy head-turner. You get the idea.

"This is another way that sewing definitely can save you money," Lundell says. "I can spend a dollar on a shirt and in forty-five minutes, it's a dress." That's cheaper than anything you'll find at a retail store—or thrift store, for that matter. Of course, Lundell points out, you have to add your time into the cost. What your time is worth will depend on how much you enjoy sewing, she adds. "The more you practice, the more you will grow to love or at least appreciate the skill of sewing," Lundell says, "but you can always start small and have a fulfilling sewing experience the first time you sit down at a machine. You first project may not be perfect—in fact, I can almost guarantee you will be using your seam ripper at least once. But perfection is not what you should be aiming for."

• HOW TO HEM A PAIR OF PANTS •

What you'll need: thread (in a color that matches the pants), scissors, marking chalk or pen, measuring tape, and sewing machine.

What to do: Fold up the bottom of the leg on the pants (inside out) until the length is where you want it. If you are hemming the pants for someone else, have him or her wear the pants for this step. If you are modifying the length for yourself, you will want to wear them and look in a mirror. After you've decided on a length, measure the distance from the fold at the bottom of the pants to the original hem. Remove the pants, turn then inside out, and place them on a flat surface. Using the measurement from before, mark with chalk or pen a dotted line where you want the new hem to be. Cut the pants just above the original hem to remove the bulk. Then evenly roll the leg up until you've reached the dotted line. (Folding the fabric this way will create a sturdier hem, but you can trim more fabric off the end of and reroll if the hem is too bulky.) Press with a hot iron and place needles to hold, if wanted. Unfinished side facing you, slide hem under sewing machine presser foot. Check to make sure that only one side of the fabric is underneath the needle. Place the needle toward the upper edge of the hem and stitch a straight line around the hem. Backstitch at the end to hold in place. Repeat with opposite leg.

• HOW TO PATCH A HOLE IN PANTS •

✧ **WHAT YOU'LL NEED:** scissors, thread, ruler, pins, needles, iron, fabric for patch.

✧ **WHAT TO DO:** Select a fabric for patch that is at least as sturdy as the fabric of the item you're mending. Measure the area of the hole or rip, by width and length. Add additional inches if you want the patch to be a specific shape, such as square or rectangle. Add ¼-inch for a seam allowance. From raw edge, measure fabric for patch. Use notches to indicate width and length, and then use scissors to cut. Place fabric wrong side up. Turn side over ¼ inch and press with hot iron. With wrong side atop hole, pin patch onto pants. Take care to make sure only one side of the pant is being caught by the needle. Thread needle and begin sewing from underside of pants. You may need to scrunch up the fabric. Start at a corner and work your way around the patch, using small stitches that evenly catch both fabrics. When finished, weave thread through back of several stitches and tie in double-knot before clipping with scissors.

HOME, STYLISH HOME

A house isn't a home until there is love in it. Cliché or not, we believe it. But we also believe that love isn't the only thing you'll need to foster that feels-like-home feeling. Like it or not, the way you decorate and present your home certainly contributes to the overall ambiance of the space—and your mood and well-being too.

"You spend so much time in your home," says Caitlin Creer, a Salt Lake City interior decorator. "It is worth it to create an ambiance that feels like you. I really believe people's homes should be personal to them. They should be a reflection of what is really important to them and include things that they like and represent their personality."[1]

In the same way that clothing is often an outward expression of individuality, a home often reflects the feelings and interests of the people who live there.

Despite what you may have read elsewhere, home decorating doesn't mean spending thousands of dollars making your abode magazine-worthy. Really,

Creer says, it's about marrying form and function to create a beautiful-to-you home that works well for the way you live.

• FIND YOUR STYLE •

Back when Natalie had her first baby, she went through a phase she describes as the "HGTV junkie phase." (HGTV is short for Home and Garden Television.) One of her favorite shows was called *Find Your Style*. Each episode, an interior decorator would use a couple's style "tells" to pin down a specific definition of their style. Then she would use those magic words—country cottage or modern eclectic—to design a room that fit them to a T.

Now, you may not have a professional decorator coming to your home to tell you what's what. But putting a finger on what really suites you isn't as hard as it may seem, Creer says. Discovering what you really love will make planning and executing a design oh-so-much easier.

"There is a lot to be said for looking at magazines, design books, and blogs," says Creer, who writes her own blog at caitlincreer.com. "Just that visual exercise of looking at things will help you see what you're drawn to."

• SCRIMP AND SAVE •

Tear pages out of magazines (as long as they are yours) and download images on the web. Visit a library and leaf through interior design handbooks. Go to a bookstore like Barnes & Noble and flip through magazines. Find and read blogs by interior designers who regularly post images that resonate with you. Sign up for an account at Pinterest.com and "pin" your favorite images for inspiration.

After you've collected a cache of images, examine them for common elements. Or recruit a friend's fresh set of eyes to tell you what they have in common. Maybe all of the rooms have similarly patterned throw pillows or pedestal dining tables. It could be you're drawn to white slipcovered sofas or billowy curtains.

"Exposing yourself to a lot of different ideas is great because you'll be able to say, 'These are the things I love, this is the feel I want.' You can extract elements from those images that you can replicate on your own," says Creer.

If you still feel totally clueless, consider hiring an interior decorating for a one- or two-hour consultation.

"Sometimes it helps to have a fresh set of eyes or someone to bounce your ideas off," Creer says. "A lot of designers have access to wholesale furniture, so sometimes you would end up spending the same amount of money using the designer than doing it by yourself."

• MAKE A LIST •

After you've mapped your style—or are at least pointed in the right direction—it's time to make a plan. So, take a deep breath—and a good look at your bank accounts—and start by identifying what rooms need to be improved. If you are a newlywed or in need of practically everything, pick the room in your home or apartment that you use the most.

Next, take inventory of what you've got. Make a list of what furniture must go, what can stay, and what will do for now. "Ask, 'What are the meaningful pieces I want to hold on to? What needs to be replaced?'" Creer says.

• DAMAGE CONTROL •

A quote attributed to English textile designer William Morris says, "Have nothing in your home that you do not know to be useful or believe to be beautiful." We often use that test when assessing whether a piece of furniture or décor should go or stay. Other questions to ask include:

- ⚜ Is this broken or is it functional?
- ⚜ Do I love it enough to invest the time and money to fix it?

- ❧ Can I repair it myself or do I need to hire it out? Can I afford that?
- ❧ Can I fix the broken part(s) for less than the cost of replacement?
- ❧ Is this an antique or treasured heirloom?
- ❧ Do I actually use this or is it simply taking up space?

Unless you are a whiz with woodworking, you'll likely want to donate items that are splintered, shattered, or unstable. Other unwanted pieces can be donated to charity.

• LIPSTICK JOB •

If an item is functional but less than fun to look at, a new coat of paint may be just what it needs, says Creer. "I am a big fan of breathing life into older furniture," she says. "Often, you can find really well-made, solidly constructed pieces for a great price." If you love the line and it is in good shape, a coat of paint can really update the look. Keep that mind as you inventory your house.

• BEWARE THE BOTTOM LINE •

After taking a good look at what you need or want to replace, set a budget. And it doesn't have to be a lot. Too many people equate decorating with lots of dollar signs, says Creer, who has gussied up rooms for as low as five hundred dollars.

To be sure, polishing up your pad is bound to cost you something. But you shouldn't have to sell your firstborn. "Pick a budget for a room and be reasonable about what you have to spend," Creer says. "If you can't afford to do everything, pick one main piece that you want to replace that will make the biggest impact."

This is where that inventory sheet comes in handy. If you have changes you want to make in many rooms, put together a prioritized master list. Estimate how much each switch will cost. (If you are completely clueless cost-wise, visit a store whose esthetic aligns with yours and check out the price tags). Work your way down the list as you have the money.

Be realistic about what you can accomplish with your designated decorating dollars. For instance, it isn't very pragmatic to think you can pull off Pottery Barn style on a Goodwill budget.

• IT'S ALL PART OF THE PLAN •

Use the inspiration images, budget, and inventory list to create a design plan for the room. If you're ambitious, you could cut pictures out of magazines and catalogs and pin or tape them to a piece of poster board, grade-school style. Or you could copy and paste images into a word processing document. A third option is to use a free online service like Pinterest.com.

• START SCHEMING •

At this point, you can create a color scheme and design plan. There really is no limit on the number of colors you can combine in a space, Creer says, although it can be hard to balance and coordinate a handful of colors if you haven't had much practice.

"People hear these weird decorating rules and get them stuck in their head," she says. "Someone told me that they heard that you should do your color in percentages. Fifty percent in main color, thirty percent in an accent color, and so on. I've also heard that you can't mix brown and black."

There isn't such a thing as the decorating police—unless you're crazy enough to put your house on RateMySpace.com or another HGTV show where viewers and designers rip your place apart. Otherwise, you're safe from scrutiny, and Creer says the only rules you should follow are the ones that work for you.

If you're looking for a general guideline, though, try three or so colors in a room. It may be helpful to think of a palette in terms of the overall space. Linking every room in the house together through the use of color does help give a cohesive look, Creer says. And it will likely help avoid jarring guests who would find a Day-Glo green bathroom in your otherwise neutral pad.

• COLOR YOUR WORLD •

Identifying colors that you like will probably be relatively easy. Finding a paint color will not.

"Most people go way too intense with colors," says Creer. For instance, she says accent walls are done wrong about 80 percent of the time. People choose colors that don't complement the overall scheme of the house or go way too bold in their selection.

"Just because you like it on the paint chip doesn't mean it will look good in your home. Test paint colors. You can get a sample for around five dollars, and it is well worth the money."

Otherwise, you risk painting a room yourself or hiring out the job only to discover that you despise the color. "People live with things they don't like all the time because they weren't thoughtful enough about it in the first place."

Natalie and her husband once painted a small powder room a very bright (and very ugly) tomato red. She knew she hated the color before the paint dried, but the tall and narrow space was so difficult to paint that Natalie didn't say anything. They lived with the color for a year or so, until Natalie repainted the bathroom when Todd was on a business trip. Similarly, Elyssa chose a rich cocoa-brown color for her basement—a color that looked beautiful on a paint sample. She realized it was too dark only after the paint had dried.

• BE BRAVE, NOT BEIGE •

On the opposite end of the color spectrum are homes that are too bland. Caitlin once had a client who used the family room paint color to purchase a sofa. Then, she used the same paint chip to select carpet for the room. The result was an entirely beige box.

"You can do tone-on-tone or neutral colors without having everything match exactly," Creer says. "You don't want your sofa and you walls and your flooring to be the same color. That is not design; that is not decorating."

Remember that at least some variation in color is necessary to create depth and interest in a space.

• Come Together •

If you're using several colors in a room, seek out one or two items that feature the entire palette.

"You need at least one thing that brings everything together and ties up all the loose ends," Creer says. "It can be a quilt, a pillow, a chair, curtains, or art—whatever you find that will make the room make sense."

• Gotta Love It •

When planning a design, make room for at least one item that you cannot live without. "Every room in your house should have a least one piece that you really love," Creer says. "That could be a piece of furniture, a pillow that you really love, or a piece of artwork."

Even if you can't stand pretty much everything about the room, having just one piece you love can really improve your overall attitude toward the space.

• Get Real •

Determining the specific furniture you need in a room is a fairly personal decision. Some magazines and manuals list specific must-haves for each room of the house. These can be handy references for figuring out what you want, but the most important guide is how you use your house.

"You know what will work for you," Creer says. "For instance, if you have small kids, you probably won't want to have coffee tables. You may not want to have lamps on side tables, either. You have to adapt some of those things to your situation."

Your home should work for you, not against you. If you eat dinner 90 percent of the time on the sofa in front of the TV, then you'll likely want to purchase a coffee table you can put a plate on. Or if you religiously stick to a "no TV during dinner" rule, it won't be smart to install a TV in plain view.

This same rule extends beyond furniture to the actual assignment of a space. A retired couple wanted to rethink the way they used the rooms in their house. The couple realized they rarely sat in their kitchen to eat a meal, so they turned the eat-in area into a den. Now, the husband reads the paper and watches the news while his wife prepares dinner.

If you read a lot of books, you may want a chaise to lounge on. Watch a lot of TV? An ottoman may be just the ticket.

• SHOPPING HIGH •

Many design manuals talk about "investment pieces"—items that you spend more money on outright but have for a longer time. Only you can decide what furniture you are willing to spend more money on, but Creer says that well-made dining tables, chairs, dressers, or chests of drawers will often last for a long time.

"When you buy things that you love, they will stay with you longer," she says. "Sometimes people get in the position of saying, 'I don't love that, but I'll just buy it.' A year later, they'll say, 'It's not right; it never looked right,' and then get rid of it."

Constant quick fixes can be expensive and over time can add up to a hefty chunk of change. Creer suggests identifying good foundation pieces that can be easily repurposed. For instance, a nice dresser could also be used as a buffet in a dining room, a console in an entry, or a changing table in a nursery.

Other surefire investments are a good quality mattress set and a nice sofa. "When I got married, I wish someone would've told me, 'Buy a good sofa,' " Creer says. To maximize your investment, select a sofa with simple lines and a classic look. Avoid oversized stitching or gigantic rolled arms, or any look that is tied to a particular style, she recommends.

• DOWN LOW •

Although some pieces really are worth the money, there are plenty of items in a room that don't need to cost a mint. Creer doesn't advocate heading down to a furniture store and sourcing your entire home in one swipe of a charge card.

"You don't have to go to Pottery Barn and buy all your things there," she says. "Be creative about sourcing the items you bring to your home."

Some of her favorite spots to find furniture are garage sales, thrift stores, and online classifieds like Craigslist.com. Overstock furniture websites and discount superstores are good places to check out.

Search by style keywords, like "modern" or "Queen Anne" or "Chippendale." Try to look beyond the current paint job to see an item's true potential. Inspect in person before purchasing to make sure the furniture is in good condition.

"People need to have the attitude that the right piece could be found anywhere," Creer says. "It could be at Restoration Hardware or a yard sale. Don't discriminate about where you might look for things. Look for pieces that look more expensive than they are."

When sourcing pieces for her clients, Creer frequently shops off-the-rack stores like TJMaxx or Burlington Coat Factory in addition to high-end boutiques. Antique stores, consignment stores, and thrift stores are also fair game.

"I love shopping high and low for rooms," she says. "My goal is to make rooms feel individual, collected, and varied."

• PATIENCE IS A VIRTUE •

Be patient when scouring for your solution. Natalie searched off and on for a year before finding six chairs that worked perfectly with her kitchen table. She came close to giving up and buying new chairs that cost a hundred and fifty dollars apiece. Luckily, the chairs she ended up with were a major score at only twenty dollars each. Elyssa was about to buy new bedding to update her bedroom, but instead she found a great deal on curtains to brighten up the space.

"Just don't get anxious and buy something on a whim," Creer says. "Map out a plan of what you're looking for."

Of course, no plan should be set in stone, but it will certainly be helpful in resisting impulse buys.

Don't forget to list things you no longer want on online classifieds too. "It is a great way to earn money to buy what you really want," Creer says. Natalie agrees: Every time she feels the urge to switch up a space, she searches her house for something to sell online. She usually breaks even, cash-wise, and occasionally has money left over.

• IDEAL ARRANGEMENT •

Furniture placement can really make or break a room. But that doesn't mean there is only one way it can be done. Nearly every room can be arranged in several different ways, and it is often a case of "good, better, and best."

When placing furniture, think about how the room is most often used. Is it more functional to break the room into zones or to keep it open? Consider how traffic moves through the room. Think about specific furniture pieces to make sure you will be able to open and shut doors or drawers.

Several design books that Natalie has read recommend drafting to-scale images on graph paper of a room and the furniture that will go in it. She actually did this the last time she moved and admits that while a bit geeky, it was a very helpful exercise.

• Stretch Your Dollars •

If the budget is too tight for major changes, consider minor adjustments that make a big impact, Creer says.

"Most people have a little bit of mad money or funny money," Creer says. "Use thirty dollars to buy a new pillow for your sofa. It can make a big difference in how you feel about the room."

Revamping a piece with some elbow grease is a great way to save money. If you have the sewing know-how, you can save hundreds of dollars by making your own pillow covers, curtains, or even duvet covers. (Turn to chapter eight for more information about learning to sew.)

Even really inexpensive fabric can get pricey when you need a lot of yardage. Try searching for bed sheets, tablecloths, and other large swaths of fabric in patterns you like. Sheets can be repurposed into drapery; tablecloths into duvet covers; and pillowcases into café curtains.

• For Rent •

If you rent, funnel your funds into furniture pieces that you can take with you when you move. If at all possible, try not to buy pieces that are "perfect for the space" in favor of items that will work well in most any space.

Not allowed to paint the walls? Don't stress, Creer says. You can add color and energy through patterned curtains, cool fabrics, and original art. If you're in a long-term rental, she suggests looking into removable wallpaper, a fairly inexpensive and temporary fix.

• Art-Inspired •

Deciding what to hang on the wall and where to hang it is an ever-perplexing problem for many. Here are Creer's tips for finding art you can live with:

- Avoid generic pieces—Resist the urge to pick something up at Bed, Bath & Beyond, she says. And step away from the Tuscan landscape unless it really resonates with you.

- Go for original—Original artwork can be horribly expensive, but thanks to the advent of online craft boutiques like Etsy.com, finding unique pieces is getting much easier. "If you want a bird painting, you can search 'bird painting' and find like a thousand different options."

- Think beyond the box—Framed artwork isn't the only form of art. Mirrors are a great way to fill space, just make sure that they are reflecting an image that is pleasant to look at. Groupings of decorative plates work well in many rooms, not just kitchens. Found objects make for great conversation starters, Creer says. "There are a lot of things that can be hung on walls that don't necessarily fit the generic idea of what art is." In a boy's room she designed, Caitlin hung antique tennis rackets. In her own home, she displays antique printer boxes.

- Balance family time—Family photos really personalized a space and make it feel like home. However, it is good idea to balance personal photos with other art, says Creer. "Don't have every wall be family pictures," she says. "Try for a fifty-fifty balance."

- Religious displays—Many people love to display religious art in their homes. To do so tastefully, Creer suggests limiting it to one or two such pieces per room. LDS bookstores are one place to find religious artwork. The Church's Distribution Services also sells prints and giclées of art from the Museum of Church History and Art in Salt Lake City. (These are available at the museum and at www.ldscatalog.com.) Works from Mormon artists like Minerva Teichert are beautiful and timeless, Creer says. Black-and-white art quality photographs are available of many LDS temples. In her home, Creer has framed photos of doorknobs at the Salt Lake LDS Temple. Choose religious art that resonates with you and place it in a spot where you'll see it often.

• ACCESSORIZE, ACCESSORIZE •

If you want to embrace trends, do so through inexpensive accessories. In-vogue pillows, throws, candles, and other décor are readily available at big box stores like Target and Walmart or discount stores such as Marshalls or Stein Mart.

These items can be easily changed out when fads die or when you're ready to move on to a different look.

Seasonal accessories are another way people freshen a room's look year-round. Avoid garish or cheaply made tchotchkes (knickknacks) in favor of classic items that will represent a holiday for years to come. When Natalie started collecting Christmas decorations, her mother wisely advised her to choose a style for the embellishments. Did she want ornaments in colors and designs that were country Christmas? Happy Christmas? Modern Christmas? The sage advice has made it easy for Natalie to add to her décor over the years while still keeping the look cohesive. (For the record, she picked classic Christmas.)

• Don'tcha Know? •

Some rules were made to be broken. Others really are worth following. Read on for Creer's essential do's and don'ts:

⚜ **Do** hang pictures at eye level—Too many people hang pictures and other artwork either too high or too low, Creer says. Hung too high and you'll have to crane your neck to see what it is. Hung too low and you'll have to stoop to check it out. "Think about the height of everyone that lives in the house and try to hang pictures at eye level for most people," Creer said. However, if you are five foot six and another family member is six foot six, Caitlin recommends splitting the difference to find the right spot.

⚜ **Do** follow the "rule of three"—This guideline suggests that you can mix up to three different materials or finishes in a room while still keeping the feel cohesive. That means that not every piece of wood furniture in your house has to have the same finish. In fact, a room will be more interesting if you mix finishes, Creer says. In a kitchen, for instance, this could be a hardwood floor, stone countertop, and tile backsplash.

⚜ **Don't** get carried away with mixing patterns—"There is an art to it because you really need to vary the scale of the patterns, she says. "If you don't know what you're doing, it is hard to make it look good." Creer recommends sticking with one geometric, stripe, solid, and floral per room.

⚜ **Do** have your curtains touch the floor—"If you have curtain panels, they should go all the way to the floor," Creer says. "Measure before you buy to make sure you are getting the right size." Hang curtain hardware either right above the window or just below the ceiling to elevate the size of the window, not in no-man's land in between.

☙ **Don't** put too many small pieces in a big room—and vice versa. Undersized furniture clutters a room, while oversized pieces in a small space can really dwarf the square footage.

☙ **Do** remember lighting—So many people forget about lighting in a room. But well-placed lamps and light fixtures add so much functionality to a room. Plus, Creer says she loves to use funky lamps when decorating to elevate the look of a room. Simple gourd lamps and wooden spindle lamps are two styles you can't go wrong with.

☙ **Don't** go overboard on throw pillows—You know you have too many pillows if you're constantly tossing them aside to sit on your sofa. "Throw pillow" isn't that literal of a term, Creer says, and you should be able to actually sit down with the pillows on board.

☙ **Do** stay organized—No one will notice your beautifully decorated home if there is clutter everywhere. "If you're going to spend the time and energy to make your home nice, keep it clean and organized," Creer says. (See chapter ten for more tips.)

☙ **Don't** get carried away with a theme—This is especially important in kids' rooms, where the urge can be great to select everything based on a theme. "Kids go through phases so quickly, it is like flushing money through a toilet," Creer said. "Choose pieces that are going to grow with them." If you want to purchase one or two token theme elements, like a Thomas the Tank Engine pillow, go ahead. "It's okay to make children's rooms feel childish, but if you do too much, it's going to be wasted money in the end."

☙ **Do** highlight your home's assets—Before changing anything, think about how you can highlight your houses architectural assets. Thick baseboards and door moldings could be highlighted with a bolder paint job. Long curtains can emphasize a high ceiling. If there are features you'd like to minimize, brainstorm a plan to do that too.

• INTERIOR DESIGN TERMS •

These basic terms may be helpful when coming up with an overall design concept:

- **BALANCE**—The visual weight of items that work together to create a feeling of stability. There are three kinds of balance: symmetrical, asymmetrical, and radial.

  - **SYMMETRICAL:** Relies on repeated elements to create balance. For instance, two sconces on either side of a mirror.

  - **ASYMMETRICAL:** Balance is created without duplication. Offset or dissimilar items work together to create equilibrium. One example is two chairs opposite a couch.

  - **RADIAL:** Elements radiate from a central focal point, like a spiral staircase.

- **RHYTHM**—Like in music, rhythm in design is achieved by repetition of a common element. Color is often used to create rhythm and move the eye around a room.

- **HARMONY**—The way elements combine to create an overall ambiance in a room.

- **PROPORTION**—Ratio between the size of one part of an item and another part. A good example is the relationship between a lamp shade and base.

- **SCALE**—Ratio between the size of an object and other objects in the room or the room in general. For instance, a massive ottoman and a tiny sofa.

◆ EMPHASIS—Typically referred to as a focal point, this is where the eye is meant to focus in a room. Usually the focal point is an architectural detail like a fireplace or window with a view. It can also be a beautiful piece of furniture, like a grand piano.

◆ CONTRAST—Created when two opposing elements are placed next to each other. Heightens drama and interest in a room. This can be as simple as dark throw pillows on a light color couch.

EXCESSIVE BAGGAGE
Getting Organized

Professional organizer and author Cris Evatt doesn't have a junk drawer.[1] This is stunning to Elyssa because, throughout her life, her home has had many, many junk drawers. Elyssa's a stickler for things looking clean on the surface, but the way she accomplishes that is to shove everything haphazardly into closets and drawers. This in unacceptable in Evatt's world, and from her you can learn the importance of relentlessly evaluating what "stuff" you allow to clutter your life. A lot of people think that organization is about having the perfect set of storage containers and organizing gadgets. In actuality, good Tupperware containers or shoe racks are just icing on the organizational cake. First, you have to streamline your life.

Elyssa first interviewed Evatt in 2008 for an article Elyssa was writing about organized living for a financial magazine. Evatt is the author of ten books, including *How to Organize Your Closet . . . and Your Life!* (Ballantine, 1981) and *30 Days to a Simpler Life* (Plume, 1998) with coauthor, Connie Cox.

Her career as an organizer, speaker, and author began when she "fell in love" with beautifully designed aluminum coat hangers. These, she said, first motivated her to organize her closet. Then she turned her attention to bigger things: "The closet for me became a metaphor for my whole life," she says. One of the most striking things about Evatt is how simple her life is—and how rich. For one thing, she lives in the San Francisco Bay Area, which is good start for anyone. But it's more than that. She isn't running around in a million directions the way most people are, and her home and life aren't so overburdened with material possessions that she is working frantically to afford and care for them. She limits her daily to-do list to a handful of things that have true meaning to her. She does yoga, eats fresh fruits and vegetables, sees movies, spends time with good friends, and enjoys her six-hundred-square-foot, red-shingled cottage and few possessions.

One of the most basic keys to the good life, says Evatt, is to learn live with less. "You get to the point where you don't want a lot of stuff in your life because you realize how stressful it is to take care of it," she says. It's a sentiment echoed by Connie Cox, who coauthored *30 Days to a Simpler Life* with Evatt. "Living below your means is the most important thing you can do in terms of having a simple life," she says. "The less you own, the less you have to pay for."[2]

Latter-day Saint Church leaders have frequently counseled members to stay out of debt and to live within their means. In the Church's *All is Safely Gathered In: Family Finances* pamphlet (you can find it on the website www.providentliving. org), leaders state: "Spending less money than you make is essential to your financial security. Avoid debt, with the exception of buying a modest home or paying for education or other vital needs. Save money to purchase what you need. If you are in debt, pay it off as quickly as possible."[3]

One of the most basic keys to an organized home and life is to limit the amount of stuff—of *clutter*—that you acquire in the first place. "The thing that complicates life most is clutter," said Evatt, who admits to being a bit obsessive about going through her home and getting rid of stuff she doesn't use or love. (She and Natalie are kindred spirits; Natalie loves—loves!—to de-junk.) Now, unless you are a professional organizer, you probably have a junk drawer (or two or three) and closet that are going to need tackling, and we'll get to that in a minute. But the most important first step is to not acquire "junk" in the first place.

The problem is that junk rarely appears to be junk when we first purchase it. Elyssa is a sucker for TV ads and is surely every advertising executive's dream. She can see an ad for a jalapeño-bacon-pepper-onion-ring-barbecue-meatball-cheeseburger-burger on TV and swear that she will stop at nothing to have it. It's worse if something is on sale, and heaven help us all if it involves shoes or handbags. Somewhere between the Great Depression and the twenty-first century, we Americans decided that to have worth we constantly needed new cars, new clothing, new houses, new "stuff." The problem is that this creates waste, clutter, and an endless cycle of consumerism that means way too many hours spent working to afford and house all that stuff, and not nearly enough time to do things we love and serve others.

In some way, college students and newly married couples have an edge on the rest of us. If you are living in a tiny apartment and subsisting on a meager income, you may not feel an all-consuming need to purchase an abdominal-exercise machine because there is simply no place to store it. And no money to buy it with. Although houses and incomes tend to get bigger as time goes by—at least for a while—the good habits you establish when you are young can carry with you for the rest of your organized, uncluttered life.

• DO YOU REALLY NEED IT? •

One of the best things to do before you acquire something—anything—is to figure out if you really, really need it. It's a learning process, for sure, but here's what we suggest doing before you buy something: See if you can go a week without it. Say, for example, you suddenly get the urge to host a party and serve panini sandwiches. Well, if you love this type of food and are always saying to yourself, "If only I had a melted Italian sandwich right now," perhaps a panini press is in order. But if, on the other hand, it's a decision you make on a whim, for a one-time event, there's no need to clutter your pantry with a gadget that will collect dust and take up space. Call around and find a friend or ward member with a panini maker or improvise and serve something else.

You can use a modified version of this when you are shopping for clothes as well. Always go with a list of what you need. Try on anything you think you might want to purchase, and if the price is right and you feel like a million bucks in it, buy it. If you can't decide whether or not to buy something, you have your answer: no. If you go home and are still thinking about that item a day or two later, you can always make a trip back to the store. If the item is gone, shrug and tell yourself that it wasn't meant to be. And if it's there, you'll know you really wanted it. As a shopping fail-safe, try to only shop at stores with a good return policy. Save all of your receipts—it's nice to keep them in envelopes or file folders marked by months—and keep tags on clothing until you've had a chance to try the item on again at home. When you get home, make sure you love the item as much as you did in the store. If you don't, back the clothing goes. It doesn't matter how good a deal something was. A sweater on sale that you are never going to wear is not a bargain.

Evatt and coauthor Connie Cox suggest an extreme but telling exercise for "serious simplifiers" in their book.[4] They suggest going a month without purchasing anything but perishables—items that can be consumed quickly such as gas, toiletries, and food. During the month, you should write down the things you need or want. At the end of the month, you can then evaluate whether those items really were needed. It's a great exercise, one that will teach you how many things you can happily live without. You could also do a modified version of this exercise for a two-week or even one-week period.

The key is to be relentless about what we allow to come into our lives, says Evatt. Learn to live with less, cultivate minimalism as a virtue, and enjoy the peace and serenity that comes from an uncluttered home and existence.

• GETTING ORGANIZED •

So you have both a panini maker and a bunch of sweaters you bought on sale. And, if you are like most people, not enough room to house those items. It's time to go through your living space and separate the things that you use and love from the things you don't.

Some people want to organize everything they own in one (very long) weekend. If you have help and a big project to tackle—like a storage room or a garage lined floor-to-ceiling with bins—it's a great idea to set aside a weekend to dive in. Elyssa and her husband organized their storage room together one Saturday, but for smaller projects, she finds it easiest to stick to one organizing project a day. Go through a couple drawers or one closet in an hour and then call your work good. Natalie and a good friend often take turns helping one another with organization projects. They chat and laugh while working, and it makes the jobs much more fun.

Evatt suggests that a good kick-off exercise is to fill a shopping bag with stuff you no longer need and donate it to a thrift store. This simple act will show you how easy it can be to declutter life and can inspire you for the projects to come.

• WHY KEEP CLUTTER? •

The reasons we hang on to junk are as varied as the people hanging on to it. Perhaps an item was a gift or an expensive, but entirely wrong, purchase. Maybe you think it will go up in value someday, or that you may need it in some future lifetime. Emotionally letting go of "stuff" is a hundred times harder than actually sorting through it. Elyssa has found it helpful to ask, "How does this enrich my life?" with every item she is considering keeping. If she can answer the question quickly, the item stays, if she can't, she thinks it is probably best to donate it. Remember that donating items to a thrift store or service organization will allow other people a chance to inexpensively acquire items they may truly be lacking.

For example, why keep a box of old dishes in your storage room when someone else could be using them?

• START SORTING •

Whatever you are organizing, Evatt suggests putting things in the three following categories:

- ✤ **SAVE:** These are things you know you use and love, says Evatt. Most of the items in this category will be placed there without hesitation. You are certain that you want to keep them.

- ✤ **RECYCLE:** These are items you know you don't need or want anymore. You are certain that you want to get rid of them. Gather them up to take to the nearest thrift store.

- ✤ **STORE:** This is for items that you aren't sure about. You probably don't really need these items, but for some reason you aren't ready to part with them. Maybe an item is broken. If so, repair it promptly or give it to someone who can repair it. Maybe you have a sentimental attachment a bunch of items from a specific period of your life. If so, consider choosing one item as representative memorabilia, and recycling the rest. (If, for example, you have a bunch of old T-shirts from your high school volleyball team, why not save one and donate the rest?) As Evatt and Cox say in their book, "Learn to balance to the weight of the past against the lightness of the future."[5] This is a category where you need to set your emotions aside and be ruthless. If you are hanging onto something because it was a lot of money—but a bad purchase—why keep it around to remind yourself of the mistake? If something was a gift but you simply don't like it or use it, extend the spirit of generosity in which it was given by giving it to someone who does have a use for it. (If it is truly hideous, save it for a family white elephant party.)

Of course, there are some items in the "store category" that you aren't ready to get rid of. Evatt suggests boxing them up and putting them in storage to practice living without them. Once sufficient time has gone by and you haven't needed or thought of them, you may be ready to pass them on to someone else.

After you've recycled or stored everything in the appropriate piles, it's time to put away what you are saving. It's important to store things as close to where they are used as possible. This will keep your house clean and your life simple. Take advantage of the inherent laziness in human nature and keep things in the area where you need them. For example, have an "exit area" close to the exit of your house where you can easily store and sort the things you take out of your house (purse, keys, wallet) and the things you bring in.

Another basic organization key is to group like items together, says Evatt. This is where storage containers can come in, to help you separate items and keep like things in the same place.

The most basic key to a clean house is this: Have a place for everything. When everything can be neatly and easily put away, clutter control is a snap. Here are some other suggestions from Cris Evatt and Connie Cox on simplifying specific areas of your house. Many are mentioned specifically in their highly useful book, *30 Days to a Simpler Life*.

      ✎ **DÉCOR:** Go for oversized furniture and big decorative pieces that make a statement. Keep small knickknacks to a minimum. Generally, most items smaller than a breadbox just add to a feeling of clutter.

      ✎ **BEDROOM:** Create a peaceful bedroom by removing the television, excess reading materials (like stacks of books or magazines), and work-related materials. If you are in a small space and have to store items under you bed, make sure they are stored neatly in appropriate containers, not shoved haphazardly underneath.

      ✎ **CLOSET:** In your closet, ruthlessly evaluate your clothing and discard anything you haven't worn in the past year. Get rid of stuff that doesn't fit you at your current weight, with the exception of maternity clothes for women who are in the childbearing stage of life. (These should be kept in storage to maximize the room in your closet.) Install extra hooks for accessories like jewelry, scarves, and purses. Keep a drawstring bag in the closet for dry cleaning, and invest in high-quality hangers.

∽ **BATHROOM:** In the bathroom, go through toiletries and makeup and discard anything old, used up, or unusable. (Do you really need that three-year-old blue mascara?) Cut down on your nail polish collection, and see if you can simplify the number of beauty and hygiene products you use. For storage, group like objects together where they are used. Find organizers for your drawers. (Evatt suggests even using silverware trays or desk-drawer dividers). Clear off the toilet tank, windowsills, and countertops.

∽ **KITCHEN:** Go through your cupboard and toss old and unused spices and seasonings. Streamline the amount of plates, cups, and utensils—keeping only what you really need. In cupboards, store the stuff that is least-often used in the harder-to-reach places. You want easy access to the things you'll need daily. Clean out your refrigerator once a week—it's not a place to store nearly empty ketchup bottles indefinitely. And have no pity on unused appliances—anything you haven't needed within the past year needs to go.

∽ **OFFICE:** Have a mail-sorting station set up near a trash can. Throw junk mail away, keep a basket somewhere in the house to store newspapers and magazines your family will read. With important mail, address anything that needs to be taken care of immediately, keep a separate folder for bills (to further simplify, set up everything you can to be paid automatically through your banking account), and one for "pending" items that need to be taken care of quickly. You may also want to keep a separate folder to store grocery ads and coupons in. Instead of piling papers on your desk, file them in a filing cabinet for easy access. Keep a well-stocked supply drawer (extra tape, batteries, sticky notes, paper clips, and so on). Remember, the great key to organization is to group like items together.

In short, be obsessively careful about things you buy in the first place, says Evatt. And then relentlessly evaluate the items you do have, getting rid of anything you don't need or love. The items that remain should be well-organized with like items grouped together, kept by the place they are used. When you are ready to organize, beautiful, useful storage containers can be a reward for all of your other efforts. Use the money you save not buying extra junk, and the time you save not worrying about maintaining it, for some quality interaction with your family.

DIRTY WORK
Cleaning

Make a clean sweep. Get down and dirty. Clear the air. Whichever idiom you prefer, it is time to talk dirty about getting your house clean.

Cleaning is, without a doubt, one household chore most people love to hate. Neat freak, slob, or somewhere in between, most people know cleaning is important. But awareness doesn't get the job done.

So that is where this chapter comes into play. We're here to bridge the disconnect between knowing and doing by demystifying the process of cleaning a house. After all, cleanliness is next to godliness. Read on for our advice on taking your house to the cleaners.

• CLEAR AS MUD •

One of the most maddening things about cleaning is that it can be easy to feel like you're never done, or that you'll never be caught up.

A friend of Natalie's once pointed out that some days, her life was a lot like the children's book *If You Give a Mouse a Cookie* (Numberoff, HarperCollins).[1] In the book, a mouse is offered a cookie. When he has the cookie, has asks for milk to go with it. Then he wants a napkin to wipe his face, and heads to the bathroom to make sure he doesn't have a milk moustache. His reflection reminds him that he needs a haircut, after which he has to sweep the floor. In this fashion, the mouse jumps from one activity to another, until he is again in the kitchen, thirsty for milk. Finally, he remembers he wanted a cookie.

Likewise, this friend said she occasionally went from task to task around her house, starting at least a dozen jobs without seeing a single one through to completion. While cleaning attention deficit disorder isn't harmful (or diagnosable), it is certainly exhausting. Do it too many times, and you may start to feel defeated. Like you can never get anything done.

The best way to avoid playing musical housework is to stick to the plan. And to stick to a plan, you need to have a plan.

• KISS OFF •

The well-known acronym KISS—short for Keep it Simple—Sister (our interpretation), is a good reminder to keep things as straightforward as possible.

In our opinion, the best way to make things simple is to develop a routine that works for you and stick to it. Do it so often that it becomes automatic. Soon, you won't have to burn precious brainpower trying to remember when you last cleaned the toilets and instead you can just get it done. Minutes saved add up to hours conserved. With the extra time you can do something that is actually fun, like giving yourself a pedicure, or meaningful, like organizing a family service project.

• METHODS FOR THE MADNESS •

We're not going to tell you there is only one way for clean a house, because that simply isn't true. Here are the pros and cons of a few of the more popular practices we've found. Note that these suggestions are intended for routine cleaning only.

⌐ SPEED CLEANING OR TEN-MINUTE CLEANING

Proponents of this method set a timer for ten or fifteen minutes at a certain time of the day, like right before bedtime or immediately following breakfast. While the clock is ticking, they scrub and shine furiously and frantically. When the time is up, the cleaning is finished.

- **PROS**: It doesn't take up a lot of time. It's flexible because you can focus on what really needs to be done.

- **CONS**: There's no order to how and when spaces are clean. It can be hard to adequately clean in such a short time frame.

⌐ JOB A DAY

Divide your house into sections (typically by room) and clean a different area every day, Monday through Friday. You could do bathrooms on Monday, the kitchen on Tuesday, laundry on Wednesday, and so forth.

- **PROS**: The schedule makes it easy to remember what you've cleaned last. Everything gets cleaned at least once a week.

- **CONS**: You're scrubbing something every day.

⌐ ALL IN ONE

Reserve three or so hours once a week to clean the house from top to bottom.

- ❧ **PROS**: The entire house is clean at once. You only have to wear cleaning clothes once a week.

- ❧ **CONS**: You have to dedicate a larger chunk of time to the process. And you must be able to move quickly from room to room.

ᖇ INDEX CARD CLEANING

Write all of the cleaning jobs in your house in index cards. During your dedicated daily cleaning time, pull a few cards from the pile and accomplish those cards. Don't put the cards back until the job is done.

- ❧ **PROS**: It's nice to have prompts about what needs to be done. Switching up the routine helps cut monotony.

- ❧ **CONS**: Randomness may throw you for a loop. It's hard to prioritize jobs.

ᖇ GO DEEP

Back in the day, many homemakers espoused the idea of spring-cleaning. You know, that time during April or May when you clean your house inside and out for days (and days) on end.

Although we love the so-clean feeling of sparkling baseboards and washed-down walls, spring-cleaning isn't a practical concept for today's busy households. Families, jobs, and other obligations make it hard to devote half of a month to sprucing your place up. All of the (few) times Natalie has attempted spring-cleaning, she has been so spent that she shuns chores for at least a few weeks afterward. Then her house falls apart like a house of cards, and all of her hard work was for naught.

We like a method of deep cleaning used by veteran homemaker and self-proclaimed clean freak Diane Hansen.[2] Decades ago, the Centerville, Utah, mother and grandmother developed a routine for incorporating bigger tasks into her weekly cleaning so she could avoid spring-cleaning. Her system works so well that she has taught it at Relief Society meetings and shared it with friends, family, and strangers.

"I'm an organized thinker, and I don't like clutter, so I don't work well in a messy environment. I conceived this idea years ago when I decided I didn't like the idea of spring-cleaning," Hansen says.

Hansen took a piece of paper and listed the twelve months of the year across the top. She divided the areas of her home into six areas, wrote those down the side of the paper, and assigned each area to two different months. (Her areas are kitchen, bathrooms, bedroom, family room, front room, and storage room). Each month, she reserved one or two full days to deep cleaning the designated area.

"When the beginning of the month rolled around, I thought about what I needed to concentrate on in that room, as in touch-up painting, rearranging furniture, cleaning the carpets, and such," she said.

If furniture in the room needed to be updated or flooring replaced, Hansen would do it during the month.

Her approach works well because it eliminates constant fretting about when a certain cleaning job is going to get done. For instance, every time Natalie walks up her staircase, she sees a patch of paint that needs to be touched up and makes a mental note to touch it up . . . sometime soon. Similarly, Elyssa has been meaning to scrub and organize the shelves in her kids' play room. She's going to do so, if she ever has a spare minute after doing her weekly list of regular chores.

"This has helped me be more efficient in my weekly cleaning and lighten up a bit," Hansen says. "I don't have to worry about what I haven't done because I know it will get done when its time rolls around."

• FIRST IN LINE •

Hansen likes to tackle her monthly cleaning projects at the beginning of the month. Otherwise, the days will get away from her. Although she has a task list for each room, it's not all dirty work. She also includes jobs like adding new décor or sprucing up furniture, so there is an even bigger payoff when the chores are done.

Her job chart for nearly every room includes dusting and washing light fixtures, cleaning carpets or floors, dusting and cleaning blinds, laundering curtains, oiling woods, washing walls, and vacuuming behind and rearranging furniture.

• Dismiss Distractions •

Make sure you truly set aside time to clean. Don't plan doctor appointments, run errands, or ring up a chatty neighbor. Hansen says she turns off her cell phone and quiets the ringer on her home phone, so she isn't distracted by calls.

Clean as soon as you can in the morning and before you get ready for the day. Work your way through your routine, cleaning always from top to bottom. Always dust before you vacuum, lest you direct dust mites onto your freshly cleaned floors.

• Area Authority •

We both hate it when we clean a room but pass over a crucial element. Here is a detailed by-the-room cleaning guide, built on Hansen's system. (Feel free to ignore anything that strikes you as way too over the top.)

KITCHEN

Daily:

- Unload and load dishwasher.
- Wipe stovetop if messy.
- Hand-wash dirty dishes as needed.

- Wipe down countertops.
- Sweep floor. (You may do this multiple times a day if you have small children or pets.)
- Wipe tabletop.
- Take out garbage and replace liner.

Weekly:

- Scrub kitchen sink.
- Spot clean chairs, including under booster seats or high chairs if you have them .
- Mop floors.
- Toss expired food from refrigerator. (We recommend doing this the night before trash pickup so moldy food doesn't fester.)
- Clean any visible spills in fridge or freezer.
- Spot clean top and sides of garbage receptacle.
- Clean stovetop.
- Clean microwave.

Twice a year:

- Clean and disinfect garbage can.
- Clean oven using self-clean function (Plan to do this at night when people are least likely to be in the kitchen because it can be quite smelly.)
- Pull out and clean behind oven, including sides of cabinets and floor underneath.
- Degrease backsplash.
- Wipe down small appliances, like toaster or blender.
- Pull out and clean behind refrigerator. Remove all food from

refrigerator, tossing nearly empty or unused items as you go. (Wash fridge drawers and shelves in warm, soapy water. Do not put them in the dishwasher.)

- Remove bottom rack from dishwasher and clean any gunk from drain area. Use vinegar rinse (read on) to disinfect.

- Clean inside of all cabinets and drawers. Pay special attention to crumbs and hardened food. Toss stale or past-good pantry items. Donate unused appliances and kitchenware. Reorganize cabinets if necessary. Dust and spot clean outside of cabinets with damp rag.

- Buff faucet and knobs.

- Clean blinds and/or curtains.

- Wash walls or spot clean grease marks.

- Seal countertops, if necessary.

- Clean windows and windowsills.

- Dust and wipe baseboards, moldings, and doorframes.

- Clean doorknobs and light switches.

✎ BATHROOMS

Daily:

- Hang towels to dry.

- Keep toilet paper stocked.

- Wipe visible spills on counters or spots on mirrors.

Weekly:

- Clean mirrors.

- Wipe down countertops.

- Sweep floor and mop if necessary.

- Take out garbage and replace liner.

- Disinfect and clean toilet bowl, tank, seat, and body. You may need to do this more often if young children in your house. Elyssa cleans hers almost every day because she has two young sons.

- Scrub bathtub and shower.

- Restock toilet paper.

- Launder towels and bath mats.

- Wipe down windowsills and blinds if needed.

- Clean doorknobs and light switches.

Twice a year:

- Scour shower surround to remove water and soap scum

- Clean bathtub, tackling rings or rust marks. Scrub jets in spa tub, if you have one.

- Spray shower curtain with vinegar or run through washing machine.

- Soak showerhead in vinegar to remove hard water stains, if necessary.

- Clean inside all cabinets and drawers. Throw way old toothbrushes, broken hair elastics and the like. Dust and spot clean outside of cabinets with damp rag.

- Wipe down towel bars, hooks, and doorknobs.

- Launder bath mats if not done weekly.

- Clean blinds and curtains.

- Clean windows and windowsills.

- Dust and wipe baseboards and moldings.

- Clean doorknobs and light switches.

⌒ BEDROOMS

Daily:

- ⚘ Open windows to freshen room.
- ⚘ Make bed, airing out and tucking in bed sheets.
- ⚘ Put away clutter and tidy nightstands.

Weekly:

- ⚘ Dust furniture, including picture frames and wall hangings.
- ⚘ Vacuum or sweep floors.
- ⚘ Launder sheets and pillowcases.

Twice a year:

- ⚘ Clean carpets or rugs.
- ⚘ Pull out and vacuum behind and underneath bed, side tables, and dressers.
- ⚘ Flip or rotate mattresses.
- ⚘ Clean blinds and/or curtains. If you have blinds in your bedrooms you may want to dust them monthly to reduce allergens in the air.
- ⚘ Dust and polish furniture.
- ⚘ Dust lampshades and buff bases.
- ⚘ Launder all bedding, including mattress covers, duvets, duvet covers, comforters, coverlets, and quilts.
- ⚘ Clean out and reorganize dresser drawers.
- ⚘ Go through closets, donating unused, out-of-style, or ill-fitting clothing.
- ⚘ Clean windows and windowsills.
- ⚘ Dust and wipe baseboards and moldings.
- ⚘ Clean doorknobs and light switches.

❧ FAMILY ROOM AND FRONT ROOM

Daily:

- ❧ Put away clutter.
- ❧ Clean up spills or other messes.

Weekly:

- ❧ Dust furniture.
- ❧ Dust and clean TV screen (follow TV manual directions).
- ❧ Vacuum carpets or rugs. Sweep and mop hardwood or tile floors.

Twice a year:

- ❧ Clean carpets or rugs.
- ❧ Dust and polish furniture, including picture frames and wall hangings.
- ❧ Pull out and vacuum behind and underneath sofas, chairs, side tables, and other furniture.
- ❧ Dust lampshades and buff bases.
- ❧ Launder throw pillow covers or spot clean pillows without inserts.
- ❧ Machine wash blankets or throws.
- ❧ Clean out and reorganize bookshelves, cabinets, or consoles.
- ❧ Clean blinds and/or curtains.
- ❧ Clean windows and windowsills.
- ❧ Dust and wipe baseboards and moldings.

❧ STORAGE ROOM

Daily:

- ❧ Take items to storage room, as needed.

Weekly:

- ❧ Check quickly for rodents or bugs.
- ❧ Put away open bins.

Twice a year:

- ❧ Sweep floor and mop if necessary.
- ❧ Take inventory of food storage. Note items that are expiring soon or running low.
- ❧ Make sure storage boxes are properly labeled and sealed.
- ❧ Reorganize storage boxes, leaving frequently used items accessible.
- ❧ Clean blinds and curtains.
- ❧ Clean windows and windowsills.
- ❧ Dust and wipe baseboards and moldings.
- ❧ Clean doorknobs and light switches.

❧ OFFICE

Daily:

- ❧ Put away clutter
- ❧ Sort through mail, recycling junk mail and shredding items with sensitive information

Weekly:

- ❧ Dust furniture, including computer and printer
- ❧ Vacuum carpet
- ❧ Take out garbage and replace liner
- ❧ Empty paper shredder

- ⚜ Vacuum carpets or rugs. Sweep and mop hardwood or tile floors.

Twice a year:

- ⚜ Clean carpets or rugs

- ⚜ Dust and polish furniture, including picture frames and wall hangings

- ⚜ Pull out and vacuum behind and underneath desks and chairs

- ⚜ Clean out and reorganize bookshelves, cabinets, or consoles

- ⚜ Clean blinds and curtains

- ⚜ Clean windows and windowsills

- ⚜ Clean doorknobs and light switches

• ONE TRUE THING •

Whatever cleaning routine you choose, also pick one task to do every day, no matter what. Natalie doesn't leave her house in the morning until her bed is made. Even when she is sick, she'll get out of bed to make then it and then get back in. Elyssa loves to clean—she's a bit of a freak—and usually spends a "happy hour" after she gets up making beds, emptying the dishwasher, putting away any clutter, and generally making sure her house is spic-and-span for the day to come.

It may seem silly to have seemingly trivial nonnegotiables, but the imperative ties back to an academic hypothesis know as the Broken Window Theory.[3] Introduced in the 1980s by two social scientists, this theory speculated that monitoring and maintaining urban environments could prevent further vandalism or escalating crime. Translation: If broken windows were left as is, people would perceive no one cared about the neighborhood and crime would go up. If windows were fixed, would-be criminals may be deterred.

Why are we talking about social assumptions? Because the idea can be easily applied to house cleaning.

Hear us out: When Natalie doesn't make her bed in the morning, extra pillows and shams get left on the floor. Then, when she brings in laundry to fold, she puts the basket on the floor, instead of on a freshly made bed where she can tackle it immediately.

With pillows and baskets on the floor, her kids think the bedroom is a playroom and decide to jump on the bed or toss laundry out of the hamper. In a matter of minutes, her bedroom spirals into a huge mess.

This can easily happen with entry consoles, kitchen tables, or that one spot on your countertop where things tend to pile rapidly. Of course, it would be nice if we could never leave a job undone. But because it simply isn't possible to always take care of everything, it is nice to know that there are one or two areas in your house that will always be top-notch.

• PUT DIRT IN ITS PLACE •

Preventive measures are one way to minimize the amount of cleaning you need to do.

Simply put, dirt belongs outside. Keep it there by using doormats placed both inside and outside of all major entryways to your home. Politely encourage family members, friends, and other visitors to wipe their feet on the doormat before crossing the threshold.

Pick a doormat thick enough to actually catch dirt. Shake regularly to loosen whatever may have set up camp inside, and hose down regularly. Seek out indoor mats that are machine washable.

As you think of it, sweep porches, steps, and walkways to your house. This will lessen the chance of tracking the outside in.

If you have a sandbox in your backyard or at a nearby park—and children or pets that regularly play in it—teach your children to brush sand from their clothing and shoes before leaving the box. Remove shoes outside the door and quickly wipe the bottoms of feet to remove any lingering specks. (Before she instituted this policy, Natalie used to joke that there was so much sand in her house that she might as well live at the beach.)

• IF THE SHOE FITS •

One way to keep your carpets and floors much cleaner is to institute a no-shoes-indoors policy. That may seem radical, but in many parts of the world, wearing shoes past the entry of a house is a major faux pas.

Going barefoot can be hard on your feet and flooring too, so it is a good idea to wear socks or slippers instead. You can keep both shoes and slippers in a closet close to the door so you remember to switch from one to the other.

• UP IN THE AIR •

Ever opened the door to your house only to have an unpleasant odor slap you in the face? We've all been there, wondering what on earth that faint smell is and how to get rid of it.

We aren't going to lie—it could be something funky. But, more likely, your house just needs a little airing out. Think about when you last opened windows to let the breeze float through your house. Most people keep their doors and windows shut tight so nothing interferes with air conditioning or heating schedules.

Try to open windows around the house for at least twenty minutes every day. We like to do this in the morning, as we go from room to room helping our kids get ready for the day. Usually temperatures are lowest in the morning, so this works great in the spring and summer. If it is chilly outside, still open a window or two but keep them open for only five minutes or so. You may find the cold air invigorating.

· ALL TOGETHER NOW ·

Purchase a large cleaning caddy to hold cleaners and rags, and a deep bucket for mopping or jobs that require soaking. Both can be purchased inexpensively at a grocery store or superstore.

Keep the caddy where you can grab it quickly. If you live in a house with two or more levels, consider investing in more than one caddy. That way you won't need to exert energy to fetch the singular supplies. (We know it sounds lazy, but it really helps minimize excuses for not getting the job done).

In your caddy, stock:

- **CLOTHS FOR CLEANING**. We like bar-mop-style cloths that can be inexpensively purchased in bulk. White is the right choice because they can be easily bleached. When they get too raggedy, use for paint jobs or for cleaning grease.

- **CLOTHS FOR DUSTING**. Microfiber works wonders, but make sure to follow the laundering directions on the cloths. Most microfibers should be air dried to retain their original qualities.

- **RAGS FOR BIG SPILLS**. Cut up old terrycloth towels or even stained T-shirts to use when cleaning up big messes. This is a great way to reduce the amount of paper towels you use.

- **OLD NEWSPAPER PAGES**. Believe it or not, newsprint is the only thing we will use to wipe a window clean. It gives a streak-free finish without leaving anything fuzzy behind. Plus, you're reusing and recycling.

- **ALL-PURPOSE CLEANER**. For cutting through general grease and grime.

- **FURNITURE POLISH**. Spiffs up wooden furniture easily, just make sure you don't use it on wood floors.

- **GLASS CLEANER**. Removes smudges and stains from windows and mirrors.

polish

- ✤ **ROOM-SPECIFIC CLEANERS.** Things like toilet bowl cleaner or abrasive scrub.

- ✤ **REUSABLE PLASTIC GLOVES.** For protecting your hands from hot water and chemicals in cleaners.

- ✤ **SCRUB BRUSHES AND OTHER TOOLS.** Include whatever other cleaning devices you can't live without. Keep in mind that anything you use, you'll have to sanitize and maintain. Less is definitely more.

• TO MARKET •

There are hundreds of cleaning products on the market today, each vowing to make quick work of dirty work. You likely have specific products you already use, and if they work for you, keep using them. Don't waste your time, energy, and money market-testing every single toilet bowl cleaner on the market. Also, don't buy into the hype that you need a different product for each cleaning task.

• GREEN GODDESS •

For those trying to be truly frugal, make-it-yourself cleaners are far cheaper than anything you will buy at the store—even if you're nearly getting it for free with coupons. Plus, chemical-free cleaners are much friendlier to the environment and safer for homes with small children, pets, or people with sensitivities.

"One third of people in the United States have some kind of respiratory issue, whether it is allergies or asthma," says Melissa Robinson, outreach educator at the Ogden Nature Center, a 152-acre nature preserve and education center in Ogden, Utah. Classes and workshops focus on topics like art, photography, birding, conservation, and sustainability. Robinson has taught classes on nontoxic cleaning products. "That makes me want to make sure my house isn't a place where people are having respiratory issues because of the chemicals I use."[4]

There are only a few basic ingredients required for most homemade cleaners, and you will likely already have most of them in your cupboard:

- **VINEGAR.** The acid in vinegar eliminates odors, cuts grease, cleans stains, and leaves no residue. When cleaning, use only plain white vinegar, never apple cider or other varieties. Buy this in bulk at a membership "club" store, and you'll have a year's supply for only a few dollars. (Never use on stone or marble; acid will etch the surface).

- **WASHING SODA.** Made by Arm & Hammer, this has twice the strength of baking soda. It neutralizes odors by changing the pH. Find it in the laundry aisle at most large grocery stores.

- **BAKING SODA.** Like washing soda, baking soda eliminates rather than masks odors. It's great for jobs requiring an abrasive cleaner.

- **LEMONS.** This citrus fruit is acidic and also has antibacterial and antiseptic properties. It works great as a natural bleaching agent. Any basic lemon from the grocery store will do.

- **LIQUID DISH DETERGENT.** Choose your favorite. We like "pure" lines with fewer ingredients and no artificial scent. In general, the fewer the ingredients, the better it is for you.

• FREE AND CLEAR •

If you're worried these homemade solutions won't work, think back a few decades to a time when many people didn't have access to as many chemical cleaning products as we do now. Your grandma likely used a lot of vinegar and water—and some elbow grease, of course.

"If you step back, you realize these things have been used for years, and they were used because they work," Robinson says.

• RECIPES •

Ready to save some money and, perhaps, the environment? Read on for recipes:

BATHROOM CLEANER

½ cup washing soda   1 gallon warm water

Dissolve washing soda in water. Scrub areas with cleaner and rinse well. Do not use on fiberglass sinks, tubs, or tile.

SOFT SCRUB

½ cup baking soda   liquid dish detergent

Place baking soda in small bowl. Add liquid dish detergent until consistency is similar to that of a mild abrasive cleaner.

WINDOW CLEANER

½ to ¼ tsp. liquid dish detergent   2 cups water

3 Tbsp. vinegar

Combine in empty spray bottle. Use like Windex to clean mirrors, glass, and other shiny surfaces.

FURNITURE POLISH

½ tsp. oil (olive, vegetable, or canola)   ¼ cup vinegar or fresh lemon juice

Mix in a small mason jar or clean baby food jar. Dab a soft rag into solution and wipe on wood surfaces to shine.

ALL-PURPOSE CLEANER

¼ teaspoon washing soda   2 cups hot tap water

small dab of liquid soap, any kind

Combine in empty spray bottle, swishing to integrate. Use as you would an all-purpose cleaner, such as 409.

· AMAZING VINEGAR ·

Plain old white vinegar has so much more to offer beyond use in sauces, dressings, and condiments. Test it out with these ten ways to use vinegar:

1. As a rinse aid. Place vinegar in the rinse aid compartment of your dishwasher and run as usual.

2. To unclog a drain. Sprinkle a handful of baking soda down the clogged drain, followed by ¼ cup vinegar. Cover the drain with a stop for 15 minutes, and then flush with cold water.

3. Remove stains on nonstick pants. White spots on the bottom of nonstick pans are caused by minerals in the water. Rub a cloth dipped in vinegar across the stains to send them on their way.

4. Clean a dishwasher. Place one cup of vinegar on the bottom rack of an empty dishwasher. Run through a complete cycle and the dishwasher will be shiny and new.

5. Spiff up steel. Shine chrome fixtures using a cloth soaked in vinegar. Works great on bathroom and kitchen faucets.

6. Disinfect a shower curtain. Soap, shampoo residue, and mildew build up quickly on shower curtains and liners. Wipe down directly with undiluted vinegar. Or, place in washing machine and add one cup vinegar to the rinse cycle. Hang to dry.

7. De-gunk a showerhead. You could use expensive calcium, lime, and rust removers, but try vinegar first. Remove the showerhead and soak overnight in a bowl filled with vinegar.

8. Clarify hair. After shampooing hair, skip traditional conditioner and rinse with a solution made from one cup water and a tablespoon vinegar.

9. Neutralize a toilet bowl. Dump a cup of vinegar into a toilet bowl. Let stand five minutes before flushing.

10. Kill unwanted grass. Instead of using toxic chemicals to kill stubborn grass growing between concrete, try vinegar. Pour directly on unwanted grass or weeds.

• Other Au Naturel Fixes •

Use leftover citrus rinds, like those from lemons or oranges, to de-funk your garbage disposal. Just place a rind down the drain, run the tap, and turn the disposal on.

Loosen the gunk inside your microwave by putting water and a bit of baking soda in a microwaveable safe dish. Turn on the microwave for three or four minutes, or until the water boils. The steam from boiling water will make it easy it wipe the interior down.

Place an open box of baking soda in a refrigerator to absorb odors. Replace every two to three months.

Sprinkle baking soda into carpet before vacuuming to eliminate pet and food odors.

• Girls Just Wanna Have Fun •

It's worth your while to make cleaning fun. Yes, we said fun! No matter where you live, you'll likely spend a good chunk of time throughout your life sweeping and scrubbing. Since you have to do it anyway, you might as well make it fun. Hook your iPod up to speakers and blast upbeat music through the house. Treat yourself to rubber gloves with polka-dotted fabric ruffles. Natalie likes to don a frilly apron, pull up her hair, and even wear lipstick. Elyssa has a special cleaning outfit that consists of a blue Dickies jumpsuit, red bandana, and, when she really wants to channel her inner fifties housewife, high heels. (She takes them off when mopping or using chemicals, but still . . .)

Taking a few seconds to pretty yourself up will likely make you smile at the reflection you see while cleaning your mirrors. In fact, we bet you're smiling right now. See? We told you cleaning could be fun.

• PICKED CLEAN •

Can't remember what product to use on what surface? Here are a few guidelines to follow:

- ❈ **TILE OR STONE FLOORS:** A good, multipurpose cleaner appropriately diluted should do the trick. If you're scouring grout lines, then a soft abrasive cleaner and toothbrush work well.

- ❈ **WOOD FLOORS:** There are a few wood-specific cleaners that work nicely, such as Orange-Glo and Pine-Sol, or you could use a multipurpose like Mr. Clean. But remember that puddled water can warp wood over time, so use a damp cloth and clean up spills as you go. Natalie has glossy wood floors and uses a cloth to wipe away streaks as she mops.

- ❈ **COUNTERTOPS:** Because countertops are food-contact surfaces, avoid chemical cleaners in favor of a natural cleaner, like vinegar, or dish soap diluted with water if you have stone counters.

- ❈ **BLINDS:** Dust with a microfiber cloth, then clean using a damp rag dipped in warm, soapy water.

- ❈ **TUB AND TOILET:** Use a disinfectant (like Pine-Sol or vinegar), and a soft abrasive cleaner if needed.

HIGH
MAINTENANCE
Caring For Your Home

Owning your own home is both wonderful (you can paint the walls whatever color you want!) and challenging (you have to repaint when the room doesn't work in magenta!). This chapter will talk about some of the basic things you can do to maintain your home, as well as ways to keep your belongings and its inhabitants safe.

When you purchased your home, it may have come with some type of warranty, particularly if the home was new at the time of sale. A warranty typically covers construction-related problems, but it probably won't cover routine wear and tear. If you haven't already done so, be sure to carefully read your warranty and familiarize yourself with its terms and time limitations. Whether your home is under warranty or not, and even if you are renting, routine maintenance will extend the life of the space and make it more livable and enjoyable.

• KEEP IT CLEAN •

One of the most basic ways to care for your home is to keep it clean and free of debris. Follow the cleaning suggestions in chapter eleven, and make sure to keep the interior areas free of clutter. Clutter causes dust to accumulate, can cause accidents, and can prevent you from spotting small problems before they become big ones. Proper cleaning will also extend the life of the materials used to build your home. Water left on hardwood floors can cause it to buckle and rot. Mildew buildup can cause musty odors and eat away at the fabrics on which it grows. Dirty faucets and furnaces will wear out faster. By regularly cleaning your house, you can protect what is likely your most valuable asset.

In addition to regularly cleaning the interior, be vigilant about keeping up your yard and home exterior. Make sure that gutters and downspouts do not get clogged with leaves and other debris. Check them periodically to clear anything that may have accumulated. Trim back shrubs, bushes, and trees to keep them from harming the exterior of your home. If you live in a cold area, make sure to take the garden hose off of your outdoor water spigot before winter. Leaving the hose on can cause pipes to split and break and can lead to flooding, says Parley Hellewell,[1] a one-time hardware store owner and the owner of many construction-related businesses in Utah.

• FIX SMALL PROBLEMS BEFORE • THEY BECOME BIG ONES

Hellewell has seen what happens when people let small problems mushroom into large ones. For example, if a roof shingle comes off in a windstorm, it's important to get it replaced before rain or snow accumulates and leaks into your house. When paint starts to flake off the exterior of houses, wood can crack and become damaged, so it's important to repaint in a timely fashion. One of the best things you can do is to take a monthly inventory of the interior and exterior of your home, checking to make sure things are in proper functioning order. And if you notice a leaky faucet or loose electrical socket at any time during the month, fix the problem immediately.

As time goes by, here are some common maintenance problems you may run into, and how to fix them:

- If a faucet starts to drip, most likely the O-ring needs to be replaced. An O-ring is a round, rubber internal component in the faucet. If you are mechanically inclined, you can try replacing the part yourself. Every brand and model of faucet is unique, so be sure that you write down what type of faucet you have when you go to the hardware store to look for parts. Make sure to turn your water supply off before starting this project.

- If a toilet continues to run after it has flushed, you'll need to first check the flapper in the toilet tank to see if it needs adjustment. The flapper is a rubber flap that sits on the bottom of a toilet and seals over a hole in the bottom of the tank. The flapper is made of rubber, and as it ages, it can harden or crack, enabling water to sneak by. You may also need to replace or adjust the fill valve (also called the ball cock). The fill valve is a narrow tube in your toilet tank that fills the tank with water. You can purchase both of these parts at a hardware store. Be sure to turn your water supply off before beginning this project.

- If your toilet becomes clogged, first try using a plunger to force whatever is blocking it down the pipes. If the toilet continues to have problems, you can use a coil spring-steel auger or a plumbing snake to break up whatever is causing the blockage. (Depending on what's blocking the pipes, you may also have to pull the item out.)

- If sinks get clogged, you can first try using a plumbing solution such as Drano. If that doesn't work, you have other options. Often when a sink is clogged, something is caught in the P-trap, the U-shaped area in the drain pipe underneath the sink. To remove the P-trap, use a large pipe wrench to undo the fittings holding that part of the pipe together. Be sure to have a bucket underneath first to catch any liquid and debris that will inevitably fall out. If there is nothing in the P-trap, you can try sending a plumbing snake down the pipes, but it may be best to call a plumber at this point.

✤ If your pipes freeze, make sure to thaw them slowly to avoid the formation of steam. This could cause the pipes to explode. Avoid this problem entirely by making sure to keep your house heated to at least 55°F, even when you leave on vacation. Noisy pipes can be a sign that something is wrong, so be sure to have this problem addressed promptly.

• MAINTAIN YOUR APPLIANCES •

Your home's biggest and likely most expensive appliance is your furnace. Parley Hellewell notes that when it comes to maintaining things within your home, "an ounce of prevention is worth a pound of cure." Just like you change the oil in your car every three thousand miles or so, you need to periodically change the filter in your furnace. Hellewell says you may need to do it as often as once a month, but depending on the type of furnace you have, you may be able to go as long as six months. Inquire about your specific furnace at a hardware or home-improvement store. Natalie finds it helpful to buy a year's supply of filters at once, so she doesn't have to run to the hardware store every time an indicator on one of her appliances starts to blink. Also, you should have your furnace cleaned and inspected yearly.

Refrigerators should be cleaned to keep them in proper working order. In addition to cleaning the interior, you will want to periodically clean its condenser coils. These coils can accumulate dust, says Hellewell. Cleaning them off will help your refrigerator function more efficiently. Condenser coils are typically on the bottom of newer-model fridges (remove the grill at the bottom front of the fridge), or in the back on older models (pull the unit off of the wall). You can use a small brush, a broom, or a vacuum to dust these coils off.

Be kind to your garbage disposal, says Hellewell. Don't expect it to function as a trash compactor or trash can. For instance, a garbage disposal may be able to handle a few potato peelings, but if you are peeling a number of potatoes, place a plastic bag in the sink to collect the skins and toss them in the garbage. Hellewell says his store would get a lot of distress calls during the canning season as well, when people dump volumes of slippery skins down the sink and they cling to the pipes. (Natalie totally ruined her disposal with thick carrot peels.) Also, don't dump grease or a lot of greasy stuff down the drain, which can clog the pipes. Use cold water when running your garbage disposal, and keep it mind that it should be replaced about every ten years.

• IN AN EMERGENCY •

If your basement started flooding and you needed to shut off the water to your home immediately, would you know what to do? What if overloaded circuits cause you to lose power to part of your house? Would you be able to turn the power back on? And what should you do if you suspect a natural gas leak? Knowing where your home's power, gas, and water supplies are located is crucial for every homeowner. Here is a quick primer for emergencies:

⤴ TURNING OFF THE POWER

Every home has a main electrical service disconnect, most often located on a home's exterior. (In newer homes, you may find it close to the home's power meter.) This will shut off power to the whole house if you flip its switch. If you have not already done so, take time to locate this main disconnect. If you cannot find it, call your power company and ask them to tell you its location.

In your home's interior, you will have one or more power panels with circuit breakers that service individual areas. It's important to know where this power panel is located in the event you need to turn on or off power to individual portions of your house, or to your entire house. (There should be some sort of labeling in the panel telling you what each circuit does. If there is not, consult an electrician.) To shut off a circuit breaker, switch it to the off position. To reset a breaker, flip it to the off position, then flip it back on again.

Note that older homes and apartments may have a fuse panel or box instead of circuit breakers. If you do not know where your power panel or fuse box is, consult an electrician.

⏤ TURNING OFF THE WATER

There are three levels of water-shutoff valves typically located in and around a home. You can either shut off all the water coming into your home—in the event of flooding—or to a specific area, which you could do in the case of a small leak when you want the rest of the house to continue to have water. You can also shut off water to your entire house as well as your outdoor plumbing (including sprinklers). We'll talk about each below.

If you need to shut off water to a small, specific area, such as a toilet or sink, use its local shutoff valve. These valves are located near the fixtures that use them, usually directly under a toilet or a sink, for example. Find the shutoff valve and turn it clockwise to shut the water off.

To turn off water to your entire house including exterior hose bibs, you need to find the shutoff valve located near where the main water supply pipe enters your house. If you live in a cold climate, it will most often be located indoors, probably in the basement if you have one. If you live in a warm climate, it may be located just outside your home. Before an emergency happens, locate this valve and practice shutting it on and off once. You can do this yearly to make sure it does not get stuck in an open position.

To shut off culinary water at the street (if you draw your water from a municipal supply), you'll need to locate the shutoff valve by your water meter. The water meter is typically located outside near the street, often in a round cylinder at ground level. When you lift the cover of the box, you will need a heavy-duty, T-shaped wrench, called a curb key, to turn it off. You can buy this product for less than ten dollars at hardware and home improvement stores. Turn it until you can't move it any further. If you can't find your water main shutoff valve, contact your water company and ask them to come out and show you its location and how to turn it off.

Note that apartments and other rental properties may have slightly different water-shutoff configurations. You should ask your landlord how to turn off water to your rental in an emergency.

TURNING OFF THE GAS

Natural gas leaks can cause explosions and deaths, so it's important to know how to shut off the gas to your home in an emergency. The Federal Emergency Management Agency (FEMA) recommends on its website, fema.org, that you contact your gas company to learn correct gas-shutoff procedure because it can vary from area to area and home to home. "If you smell gas or hear a blowing or hissing noise, open a window and get everyone out quickly. Turn off the gas, using the outside main valve if you can, and call the gas company from a neighbor's home," says FEMA.[2] Also, if your gas has been turned off for any reason, DO NOT turn it back on yourself. This needs to be done by a professional.

• THE SAFE HOME •

One important thing you should know about maintaining your living space is how to keep yourself and others who may live in or visit the home safe. Read on for some important safety tips.

FIRE SAFETY

Make sure that you have working smoke and carbon monoxide detectors installed on every level of your home, in every bedroom, and outside each sleeping area. You should test these monthly to make sure that they are functioning properly. Also, you will need to replace the batteries every six to twelve months.

Your family should have an escape plan for evacuating the house in case of a fire, says Lorraine Carli,[3] vice president of communications for the National Fire Protection Association. (The association has a cool website with fire-safety tips. Check it out at www.nfpa.org.) Every member of the family should know at least two ways out of each room, and you should establish a family meeting point outside the home in the event of a fire or emergency. You should practice your escape plan at least twice a year, says Carli.

If you have a second story in your home, keep a ladder on the top floor in case you need to evacuate through a window in the event of a fire.

The leading cause of home fires is cooking, and the leading cause of cooking fires is unattended cooking, according to the National Fire Protection Association. Stay in the kitchen if you are broiling, grilling, or frying food. And turn off the stove even if you have to leave the room for a short period of time.

Another major cause of home fires is heating. If the place you live has a working fireplace, make sure to have the chimney and the chimney connectors inspected on an annual basis. (You can find chimney sweeps in the phone book or online to do this.) If you are using a portable or stationary space heater, turn it off if you leave the room, and before you go to sleep. Keep anything that can burn at least three feet away from fireplaces and space heaters.

Store firewood outside your home and off the ground. Do not build fires on the floor, build them on the grate or andirons.

Electrical systems and equipment can cause fires. Keep all of your home's equipment in good working order, checking for frayed cords or wiring. Don't run cords under carpet or across doorways.

Worn or discolored outlets, and sometimes flickering lights, can indicate an electrical problem. Consult a qualified electrician.

Use common sense with candles. "Obviously, a candle is an open flame, [and] it can ignite flames that burn," says Carli of the NFPA. Never leave a burning candle unattended. Extinguish candles when you leave a room or go to sleep. Keep candles at least twelve inches away from walls, curtains, decorations, or other flammable items. Keep any open flame (and matches!) away from children. In the event of a power outage, use flashlights, not candles, as emergency lighting.

∽ SECURITY

In 2008, there were an estimated 2,222,196 burglaries in the United States, with property losses totaling $4.6 billion, according to the Federal Bureau of Investigation's Criminal Justice Information Services Division.[4] Also worrisome is that the majority of break-ins show no sign of forced entry, according to Michelle L. Boykins,[5] director of communications and marketing for the National Crime Prevention Council. (The NCPC is an Arlington, Virginia–based non-profit educational group formed to help reduce crime.) There are a lot of simple things you can do to protect your home's inhabitants and your belongings. Below are some of Boykins's recommendations for home safety:

❧ It's an obvious suggestion, but one that's not always followed: Lock all of your doors and windows. Your doors should have good, sturdy locks that are both pick resistant and drill resistant. Sliding-glass doors should have an additional lock (available at hardware stores), or you can use the simple, inexpensive method of inserting a wooden dowel or a broom handle in the door's sliding track to prevent it from opening. For windows, it's best to have ones with a key-lock system, where you remove the key when the window is locked. Some companies also manufacture windows with shatterproof glass.

- Take a careful inventory of your landscaping and home exterior to ensure there are no easy hiding places for burglars. Keep your trees trimmed and away from your home. Trim shrubbery so that it is no taller than window height.

- Use lighting as a crime deterrent. There should be a light illuminating all major entrances, including the front and back door and basement entrances. Motion-sensor lights are a smart and popular option because you can program them to turn on when someone is trying to sneak around in the dark.

- Don't store spare keys on your property. "We all know of the hiding places, under the potted plants and under the welcome mat," says Boykins. Don't make home invasion easy for criminals by putting keys there. Instead, leave your spare key with a trusted neighbor.

- If you feel you need extra protection, you can invest in an alarm security system and pay a company to monitor your property. Some people also choose the lower-cost option of owning a dog. "Sometimes that bark of a dog is enough of a deterrent for people, recognizing it's not going to be easy to break into a home," says Boykins.

- Be careful what you set out on the curb. If you've bought a new computer or flat-screen TV, leaving boxes outside your home is like advertising that you have new electronic equipment in the home. If possible, break the boxes down and store them in your recycling or trash bin, and don't put them out until pick-up day.

- Plan ahead before leaving on vacation. Stop your newspaper delivery (you'll need to do this several days in advance to give carriers enough notice), and ask the post office to hold your mail. If possible, put your interior lights on timers to go off at random times throughout the day to make it appear as if you are home. Close your blinds and lock all of your doors and windows. Ask a trusted neighbor to watch and check on your house, and to be in charge of calling law enforcement should he spot anything suspicious.

⚜ Along those lines, do not mention vacation plans on social networking sites. Posting about an upcoming weeklong trip to Aruba is just notifying would-be burglars that they'll have seven days to try to break into your house, says Boykins.

A good exercise for assessing the security of your home is to pretend that you've locked your keys inside the house and need to get back inside. If you can figure out a way to get in without breaking a window, you've identified a potential entrance for burglars. You can also ask local law enforcement to come and assess the security of your home, says Boykins.

• CHILD-PROOF YOUR HOME •

Even if you don't have children, it's likely that a child or young person may visit your home at some time. Below are a few basic safety tips. If you do have small children living at home, consult a childcare book or expert for additional baby-proofing steps.

⚜ Keep matches, lighters, sharp knives, and razor blades out of reach of children.

⚜ Store medications in child-proof containers, on a high shelf in a cool, dry place that children can't access. Keep medications out of the bathroom "medicine" cabinet.

⚜ If you have guns in the home, make sure they are unloaded and locked in a secure place such as a gun safe. Store the ammunition in a locked, separate location. Do not let young children know where your guns are stored.

⚜ If you have an exercise room, lock it when not in use to keep children away from treadmills, heavy weights, and any other equipment you might have. Make sure to keep your treadmill unplugged. Remove its key after each use and store it in an inaccessible location.

⚜ Prevent scalding and burning by keeping your water heater set to no higher than 120°F.

- ❧ Keep household plants off the ground and in places children can't reach.

- ❧ Store all cleaners and chemicals in their original containers on a high shelf inaccessible to children.

- ❧ Be smart about electricity. Put plug covers in unused outlets, keep cords out of reach of children, and put away electrical appliances (anything from a hair dryer to a mixer) after use. Replace frayed or cracked cords.

- ❧ Watch out for cords on window blinds, which have loops that can strangle a child. If you do have these cords, tie them up at the top of each window when children are in the house.

- ❧ Remember that children can drown in just two inches of water. Make sure to always drain the bathtub. Keep kids away from pools (if you have one, it must have a fence with a gate that locks), splash pools, ponds, wells, and other areas of open water.

• THE ENERGY-EFFICIENT HOME •

New home construction is becoming ever more efficient and eco-friendly. If you have recently purchased a new home, it may already have water-efficient toilets and plumbing fixtures, compact fluorescent light bulbs, and low-emissivity (Low-E) windows. If you have an older home, installing these items can save both energy and money in the long run. Also, if you don't already have one, install a programmable thermostat that can turn down the heat or turn up the air conditioner when you aren't home or are sleeping.

• TOOLS OF THE TRADE •

You don't have to star in your own home improvement show to do basic maintenance around the house, but you do have to have the proper tools. A few to

229

start with are a hammer, screwdrivers (Phillips and flat-head), a crescent wrench, a level and tape measure (crucial for hanging pictures), a mallet, and a cordless drill. From there, you can add to your collection depending on your interest in home improvement and your needs.

• IN THE END •

Your home will probably be your biggest investment, and it will undoubtedly be where you spend the majority of your time. So don't just make it livable, make it a haven and a refuge, the place every member of your family always wants to be. Fix it up, clean it up, and make it smell good and look beautiful. Bake homemade chocolate chip cookies, burn scented candles (safely), and fill the halls with music and laughter. And don't forget the important quality any successful homemaker can bring to the table, and everywhere else . . .

⬩ ACKNOWLEDGMENTS ⬩

We'd like to thank all of the sources interviewed for *"Happy Homemaking"* for so willingly sharing their knowledge. We are also grateful to the Cedar Fort team for making this book possible.

⬩ NOTES ⬩

Chapter 1: In the Money

1. *All Is Safely Gathered In: Family Finances.* The Church of Jesus Christ of Latter-day Saints (2007).

2. John Brandt, telephone interview, May 10, 2010.

3. N. Eldon Tanner, "Constancy Amid Change," *Ensign*, November 1979, 81.

Chapter 2: Sweet Setup

1. Todd Leonard, telephone interview, April 20, 2010.

2. Caitlin Creer, personal interview, July 2, 2010.

Chapter 3: Perfectly Planned

1. Shandra Madsen, telephone interview, April 15, 2010.

Chapter 4: Whatcha Got Cookin'?

1. Todd Leonard, telephone interview, April 20, 2010.

2. Shelley Feist, telephone interview, April 8, 2010.

3. "Safe Food Handling Practices," Partnership for Food Safety Education, n.d., accessed April 8, 2010, www.fightbac.org.

4. "Cook Fact Sheet," Partnership for Food Safety Education, n.d., accessed July 20, 2010, www.fightbac.org/storage/documents/flyers/cook_%20fightbac_factsheet_2010_bw_.pdf.

Chapter 5: Baking Bliss

1. Jeannie Tuckett Dayton and Mindy Spencer, personal interview, April 21, 2010.

2. Ibid.

3. Rose Aldridge, telephone interview, July 10, 2010.

Chapter 6: Squirreled Away

1. *All Is Safely Gathered In: Family Home Storage*, The Church of Jesus Christ of Latter-day Saints (2007).

2. Jeannie Tuckett Dayton and Mindy Spencer, personal interview, April 21, 2010.

3. Don Pectol, telephone interview, April 28, 2010.

4. "FEMA: Water," Federal Emergency Management Agency, last modified August 11, 2010, http://www.fema.gov/plan/prepare/water.shtm.

5. Shandra Madsen, telephone interview, April 15, 2010.

6. "Provident Living: Product Recommendations," The Church of Jesus Christ of Latter-day Saints, n.d, accessed July 22, 2010, http://providentliving.org/content/display/0,11666,7531-1-4062-1,00.html.

7. Ibid.

8. "Provident Living: Packaging Recommendations," The Church of Jesus Christ of Latter-day Saints, n.d., accessed July 24, 2010, http://providentliving.org/content/display/0,11666,7532-1-4063-1,00.html.

Chapter 7: How Does Your Garden Grow?

1. "Provident Living: Growing a Garden," The Church of Jesus Christ of Latter-day Saints, n.d., accessed July 26, 2010. http://www.providentliving.org/content/display/0,11666,6637-1-3427-1,00.html.

2. Larry Sagers, telephone interview, June 9, 2010.

3. Kathleen Riggs, telephone interview, June 7, 2010.

Chapter 8: Beyond Wishy-Washy

1. Mary Marlowe Leverette, email interview, June 11, 2010.

2. Carrie Lundell, telephone interview, May 11, 2010.

Chapter 9: Home, Stylish Home

1. Caitlin Creer, personal interview, July 2, 2010.

Chapter 10: Excess Baggage

1. Cris Evatt, telephone interview, January 22, 2010.

2. Connie Cox, telephone interview, January 9, 2009.

3. *All Is Safely Gathered In: Family Finances.* The Church of Jesus Christ of Latter-day Saints (2007).

4. Connie Cox and Cris Evatt Cris, *30 Days to a Simpler Life* (New York: Plume, 1998).

5. Ibid.

Chapter 11: Dirty Work

1. Laura Joffe Numeroff, *If You Give a Mouse a Cookie* (New York: HarperCollins, 1985).

2. Diane Hansen, telephone interview, July 4, 2010.

3. George L. Kelling and James Q. Wilson. "Broken Windows." *Atlantic Magazine.* (March 1982), accessed July 7, 2010, www.theatlantic.com/magazine/archive/1982/03/broken-windows/4465/.

4. Melissa Robinson, telephone interview, July 7, 2010.

Chapter 12: High Maintenance: Caring for Your Home

1. Parley Hellewell, telephone interview, May 24, 2010.

2. "FEMA: Utility Shutoff and Safety," Federal Emergency Management Agency, last modified August 11, 2010, http://www.fema.gov/plan/prepare/utilityplan.shtm.

3. Carli, Lorraine. Telephone interview. 11 May 2010.

4. "2008 Crime in the United States: Burglary," Federal Bureau of Investigation's Criminal Justice Information Services Division, September 2009, accessed July 24, 2010, http://www2.fbi.gov/ucr/cius2008/offenses/property_crime/burglary.html.

5. Michelle L. Boykins, telephone interview, June 11, 2010.

ELYSSA ANDRUS

Elyssa Andrus has worked as a newspaper reporter and editor for more than a decade, most recently at the *Daily Herald* in Provo, Utah. A former adjunct professor of communications at Brigham Young University, Elyssa spends much of her day chasing around her three young children. It's been more than two years since any of her baked goods have exploded or caught on fire.

NATALIE HOLLINGSHEAD

Natalie Hollingshead is a former magazine editor turned freelance writer. She has a degree in print journalism from Brigham Young University. She balances work for local and national publications with her most important job yet—mom to two energetic children. Natalie has been obsessed with organizing and decorating since childhood. Her husband, Todd, often comes home to find she has (yet again) rearranged the kitchen cupboards.